Cambridge Elements ≡

Elements in Eighteenth-Century Connections
edited by
Eve Tavor Bannet
University of Oklahoma
Markman Ellis
Queen Mary University of London

PASTORAL CARE THROUGH LETTERS IN THE BRITISH ATLANTIC

Alison Searle
University of Leeds

CAMBRIDGE
UNIVERSITY PRESS

CAMBRIDGE
UNIVERSITY PRESS

Shaftesbury Road, Cambridge CB2 8EA, United Kingdom

One Liberty Plaza, 20th Floor, New York, NY 10006, USA

477 Williamstown Road, Port Melbourne, VIC 3207, Australia

314–321, 3rd Floor, Plot 3, Splendor Forum, Jasola District Centre, New Delhi – 110025, India

103 Penang Road, #05–06/07, Visioncrest Commercial, Singapore 238467

Cambridge University Press is part of Cambridge University Press & Assessment, a department of the University of Cambridge.

We share the University's mission to contribute to society through the pursuit of education, learning and research at the highest international levels of excellence.

www.cambridge.org
Information on this title: www.cambridge.org/9781108970464

DOI: 10.1017/9781108980760

First published 2023

A catalogue record for this publication is available from the British Library

ISBN 978-1-108-97046-4 Paperback
ISSN 2632-5578 (online)
ISSN 2632-556X (print)

Cambridge University Press & Assessment has no responsibility for the persistence or accuracy of URLs for external or third-party internet websites referred to in this publication and does not guarantee that any content on such websites is, or will remain, accurate or appropriate.

Pastoral Care through Letters in the British Atlantic

Elements in Eighteenth-Century Connections

DOI: 10.1017/9781108980760
First published online: August 2023

Alison Searle
University of Leeds
Author for correspondence: Alison Searle, A.A.Searle@leeds.ac.uk

Abstract: Choosing the right words is itself an act of caregiving. Centring on correspondence archives allows pastoral letters to be analysed as a distinct literary genre that contributed in complex ways to early modern practices of caregiving, negotiating political oppression, geographical isolation, and colonial experimentation. Forms of care were solicited, given, and received through the material technology of the letter as a literary artefact. The exchange of letters created new bureaucratic and pastoral structures and entanglements between Protestant believers and others across the British Atlantic and reveals the contentious balance between care and cure within early modern communities. Pastoral care involves exercising power: epistolary exchanges sustain, exploit, shape, and distort the spiritual and material well-being of individuals and communities in a landscape fissured by religious division, enslavement, and imperial expansion.

Keywords: pastoral care, letters, enslavement, literary caregiving, Richard Baxter

ISBNs: 9781108970464 (PB), 9781108980760 (OC)
ISSNs: 2632-5578 (online), 2632-556X (print)

Contents

Introduction

Pastoral care is usually experienced in community: whether in the hierarchical form of an ordained minister counselling a parishioner, or in horizontal exchanges between like-minded believers gathering for fellowship. The shape of these ecclesial structures was radically challenged and reimagined in various ways during the Interregnum creating new intersectional spaces for pastoral care. Following Charles II's restoration these freedoms were reversed, and many conscientious English Protestants were no longer able to gather in corporate assemblies. These proscribed communities adopted a range of creative mechanisms through which to nourish and sustain their personal and corporate spirituality, identities, and doctrinal convictions; sending and receiving letters was one of the most significant and pervasive of these. Though such letters exposed individuals to censorship and prosecution, particularly former clergy, as a literary genre and a technology for communication letters enabled relationships between networks of nonconformist believers to be sustained, and they facilitated the provision of holistic care.

The provision of pastoral care through letters is examined by focusing on two transatlantic case studies of correspondence: letters sent to and from the English (later nonconformist) minister, Richard Baxter (1615–91), and the correspondence of the earliest missionaries of the Society for the Propagation of the Gospel in Foreign Parts (SPG) in North America (c. 1701–20). Both archives are extensive, moving between manuscript and print, mapping England's uneven development as a nation state, its attempts to sustain a parochially organised national church, and its proto-imperial ambitions in the Caribbean and North America. Pastoral care through letters thus involved British Protestant clerical and missionary engagement with Native Americans, enslaved Africans, and indentured servants, as well as voluntary immigrants from the British Isles and continental Europe.[1] Defining appropriate objects of epistolary care was contentious.[2] The pluralistic nature of Protestantism in the early modern British Atlantic meant that in some parts of North America the English state church was disestablished and prompted Anglicans to adopt an aggressively evangelical approach to groups such as Congregationalists, Baptists, and Quakers. Equally complex was assessing the use and mediation of communication technologies with disenfranchised populations: literacy was central to how many Protestants defined Christian practice and mission, but it also threatened

---

[1] Bross, *Future History*; Fuentes, *Dispossessed Lives*; Gerbner, *Christian Slavery*; Glasson, *Mastering Christianity*.

[2] The term 'objects' of care is used to identify the ways in which an organisation can be a recipient of care (as the SPG sometimes figures), and to denote the objectification of individuals through persecution or enslavement that shapes the resourcing and provision of pastoral care.

to destabilise settler societies dependent on enslaved labour for survival. This increased the political, emotional, and financial stakes when delimiting who should (and should not) give or receive pastoral care through letters.[3]

Pastoral care, as a concept and practice, mediates between the spiritual and medical or soul and body. This Element assesses how such care has been solicited, given, and received through the material technology of the letter as a literary genre.[4] It considers what is at stake when someone writes (and gives) or reads (and receives) a letter as an act of pastoral care, and what distinguishes this from other forms of pastoral care in the early modern period, such as sermons, catechising, or in-person visits to congregational members. Letters have specific affordances that separate them from other textual technologies and centring this genre enables a reassessment of pastoral caregiving in the early modern British Atlantic including how this literary form distinctively shaped and facilitated the sustenance, well-being, and exploitation of individuals and fragile community structures. Letters, for example, were central to the establishment of the bureaucratic processes and administration of the SPG in its first two decades, fashioning mechanisms that allowed the corporate provision of pastoral care across vast geographical distances, and in the process transforming the English state church's understanding of itself and its parochial responsibilities.

Historical Context: The Early Modern British Atlantic

The spaces of encounter formed by transatlantic commerce and Christian mission generated ambivalent zones of experimentation and entanglement in the early modern period that galvanised new forms of creativity and constraint in the provision of pastoral care. This conceptualisation is designed partially to deconstruct and highlight inadequacies in the language of centre versus periphery, or simplistic win/loss models of power, when discussing community engagement, care, and forms of exchange in the historical case studies examined in Sections 1 and 2. These liminal zones of experimentation and entanglement are used to situate and assess the creativity generated either by the breakdown of, or enforced exclusion from, state structures of governance, education, and worship, or the geopolitical logistics confronting Protestant missionaries in a transatlantic context. It facilitates cross-cultural comparisons between nonconformist and conformist communities faced with shifting

---

[3] Though not the focus of this Element, it is important to note that hegemonic practices of curation have shaped surviving personal and institutional archives in ways that further problematise the task of recuperating forms of epistolary caregiving within these transatlantic communities.

[4] Black, *Reformation Pastors*; Cooper, 'Richard Baxter and His Physicians'; Newton, *Misery to Mirth*; Schmidt, *Melancholy and the Care of the Soul*.

state/church power relations and how such different forms of constraint establish a paradoxical freedom that inspired new ways of doing things, such as communal worship and the administration of the sacraments. Liminal zones also generated often discomfiting accommodations and intimacies across bodies, temporalities, and geographies resulting in the forging of new bonds, intercourse, and conceptualisations of the state that challenged and transformed ways of imagining and building the communion of saints, as well as the body corporate and spiritual, both in time and eternity. Recent intersectional scholarship, attending to gender and race, has produced compelling accounts that provide an essential calibration of how the reception and provision of pastoral care are reconstructed through the analysis of two manuscript archives from the early modern British Atlantic in this study.[5]

Ulinka Rublack identifies the need to embed analysis of Protestant practices through 'reciprocal comparison' globally, allowing each case to be viewed 'from the vantage point of the others' and thus attending 'to the experiences of indigenous people as actively producing and reproducing spiritual worlds, knowledge, and life-worlds of wider consequence'.[6] The close integration between British imperial expansion and the religious and educational mission of the state church in the late-eighteenth and early-nineteenth centuries sometimes results in the assumption that this characterised English state church practices in earlier periods too. However, the formation of transatlantic structures of care was contingent, occasionally voluntary, and experimental, shaped by the logistics of geographical distance and available communication technologies. It does not fit the template of a metropolitan campaign designed to impose the state church on territories under the English crown abroad. If anything, mission projects reveal the fractured nature of seventeenth-century British Protestantism and evidence 'the most durable vestiges of the attempt after 1660 to widen the space of the state church to reintegrate "tender consciences" stirred in the years of Civil War'.[7] Pastoral care was a central component through which these ecclesiological fissures and synergies were worked out between c. 1650 and 1720. Anglicanism was reshaped pastorally rather than politically during the short reign of the Catholic, James II, and the Revolution of 1689, and these changes to the state church eroded sharp distinctions between its practices of pastoral care and those of mainstream Protestant nonconformity.[8]

During this period expansionist projects pushed the English state church into geographical and ecclesiastical spaces in the Caribbean and North America where it was vulnerable and uncertain of its status. Letters were the essential

---

[5] Fuentes, *Dispossessed Lives*; Carby, *Imperial Intimacies*.
[6] Rublack is partially citing Merry Wiesner-Hanks. Rublack, ed., *Protestant Empires*, 11–17, 28–9.
[7] Glickman, 'Protestantism', 381.   [8] Sirota, *The Christian Monitors*, 62–5.

textual technology that allowed these new global experiments in pastoral care to work at all, due to their ability to travel, and dramatically stretched the imaginations of those participating. Brent Sirota argues that this 'increasingly capacious pastoral concern, and the promotional and organizational structures within which it was embodied, must be comprehended within the genealogy of modern British humanitarianism'.[9] If commerce justified Christian communion, then such humanitarianism 'in the first instance [is] a problem of ecclesiology':[10] benevolence and violence are intimately entangled from its inception. Christopher Codrington's bequest of two Barbados plantations, maintained through the exploitation of enslaved labour, to resource the caregiving and missional ambitions of the fledging SPG irrevocably shaped its developing organisational character and practice and brings such challenges into sharp relief. There were also constraints on what could be imagined.[11]

The British Atlantic, as a theoretical and geographical paradigm, is a central component to the argument developed here.[12] The SPG's archive was transatlantic from its point of origin, reflecting the ways in which a small, nationally defined state church attempted to negotiate the challenges that commerce with and emigration to North America and the Caribbean presented to a parochially structured ecclesial organisation. Baxter's epistolary network is also transatlantic and offers evidence of early Protestant engagement with missionary endeavours, particularly in his correspondence with John Eliot, a Congregationalist missionary to the Narragansett Indians and other Native Americans.[13] Baxter supported the work of the Company for the Propagation of the Gospel in New England (founded in 1649) and offered an early critique of European Protestants involved in capturing, enslaving, and exploiting African people in his casuistical compendium, *The Christian Directory* (1673).[14] Missionary work is an important aspect of both case studies and demonstrates how pastoral care as a point of analysis can be borne through to other areas of discussion, particularly in the development of correspondence networks and the establishment of new structures of care. As a communication technology, letters were essential to

---

[9] Ibid. 225.   [10] Ibid.

[11] For example, the way developing ideas about race shaped eschatology. Trigg, 'The Racial Politics of Resurrection'.

[12] 'The "Atlantic" therefore becomes both a category of analysis as well as a method of approach ....Unified states and nations had not yet fully developed .... Settlers in Britain's North American colonies did not live isolated, secluded lives independent of the concerns of their native land'. Colonists' writings and news 'shaped ideas, politics, and society in England'. Pullin, *Female Friends*, 23.

[13] Rosenberg, 'Thomas Tryon'; Burton, 'Crimson Missionaries'; Glickman, 'Protestantism'.

[14] Baxter, *The Christian Directory*, 557–60. Baxter's critique does not extend to a condemnation of slavery as an institution, but to this aspect of how it was practised. On forms of servitude, see Smith 'Between the Galley and Plantation'.

facilitating transatlantic commerce and communion, and the opportunities that each offered to expand the imagination of the British public through exposure to new objects and spaces for pastoral care. Correspondence networks were also integral to the material aggrandisement, exploitation, and enslavement that underwrote Britain's nascent imperial project.

The use of two case studies from c. 1650 to 1720 cuts across traditional scholarly periodisation and allows an exploration of how the letter as a genre was adapted to provide pastoral care in a time of multiple and disruptive alterations in the British religious settlement and rapid expansion of Britain's imperial reach across the Atlantic, which precipitated efforts to provide spiritual care to different categories of people. The diversity and range of pastoral correspondence in the Baxter and the SPG archives allow the impact of both these elements to be explored in detail, as they evidence the significance of censorship, persecution, and new communication routes that both enabled and constrained how pastoral care was given and received through letters in the early modern British Atlantic. Interrogating these two archives facilitates a calibrated assessment of how these changing political, religious, and communication infrastructures both emerged from and nourished the ways in which early modern subjects imagined, practised, and developed literary caregiving.

Pastoral Care

In contemporary parlance, pastoral care has become a generic term for broader support networks and caregiving structures, and spiritual care is preferred when focusing on the relationship between humans and a transcendent other.[15] In the early modern British Atlantic, however, pastoral care denotes more precisely the intersection between structures of religious authority, or cure, variously defined, and a responsibility to provide care for the souls, and sometimes bodies, of parishioners or congregants. Early modern pastoral care was personal and holistic – drawing on forensic (interrogatory) and medical (cases) discourses – and administrative or bureaucratic, both scenarios were dealt with on occasion through letters. Different circumstances could precipitate this necessity: for Baxter, it was both the inchoate period of revolution in the 1650s and enforced separation from his congregation due to his principled nonconformity following the Restoration (though letter-writing was also an important component of his pastoral caregiving practices as a parish priest in Kidderminster). For the SPG letters were essential as they built structures for administering the recruitment, training, support, and reporting of missionaries from an institutional base in London across Britain, continental Europe, North

---

[15] Speelman, 'Shifting Concepts of Pastoral Care'.

America, and the Caribbean. Innovations in the use of paper as a technology were critical to the developments in communication and bureaucracy that underwrote such epistolary exchanges, and the role of the SPG's first Secretary, Joseph Chamberlayne, was central to ensuring that global exchanges of paper packets, and their accoutrements of books and other material, was facilitated with care and efficiency.

These two archives allow Baxter and the SPG's historical practices of pastoral care to be explored and, in turn, require the analysis of pastoral care as a concept. This includes defining relationships between religious, philosophical, and scientific forms of caregiving through examining vocabularies of emotion and experience, exemplified in letters, and assessing what these letters reveal about the epistemologies shaping care provision and the role of the pastor or missionary as a physician of body and soul. These archives reveal how nonconformist and marginal Protestant communities created and maintained horizontal networks of social capital by developing epistolary vocabularies and structures that nurtured their well-being. Tracing the material history of care as a series of moments of lived encounter between pastor or missionary and congregant or the SPG's Secretary highlights the rich interrelationships between care and cure. Focusing on the material ways in which early modern communities used letters to provide care also shows how political exclusion, or geographical distance from the metropolitan centre, contributed to the increasing distinction between professional specialisations as, for example, the roles of pastor, missionary, natural philosopher, or physician.

The political and economic stakes of pastoral care were high in the early modern British Atlantic and debates about how it should be provided acted as a forum where issues of contention were vigorously explored. Baxter's correspondence preserves voices personally witnessing to monarchical and episcopal overreach, the effects of war fracturing communities, and repeated constitutional upheaval, creating political, social, and religious crises. Correspondents raise existential questions in a context where they no longer knew who to ask. This exposes the essential role of correspondence in the intellectual ferment of the early modern British Atlantic. Letters, both public and private, in print and manuscript, allowed Baxter as a minister and scholar to provide pastoral care by formulating creative theological, emotional, and political responses to the experience of revolution, and later, to political exclusion from public life. Section 1 offers a reappraisal of how Baxter's letters functioned as a mechanism of pastoral care during a period when such caregiving was inevitably contentious.

Anglican expansionist projects, following the Restoration, evidence a state church struggling with its insularity and thus represent a de-territorialisation of Anglicanism. These tensions are frequently evident in early correspondence, such as that from South Carolina, where the SPG missionaries note the success of nonconformist Protestants locally and the lack of financial and political support from their parishioners. Sirota postulates that when thinking about ecclesiastical expansion the state church adopted a primary orientation towards England's maritime and commercial empire, and this neither requires nor assumes that such 'ecclesiastical expansion proceeded with the concurrence of the state'.[16] Integral to an 'increasingly capacious pastoral concern, and the promotional and organizational structures within which it was embodied', is the way spaces of 'free association, commercial enterprise, and intersubjective communication' became imaginable as 'an alternative ecology for Christian life'.[17] The letter-writing activities of both nonconformists and Anglicans experimenting with voluntarism are central to developing a nuanced account of the sacralisation of civil society and its reimagining as 'the preeminent stage of public moral enterprises' in the early modern British Atlantic.[18] Anglican experimentation with voluntarism in pastoral care relied heavily on the cooperation of continental Protestants, with whom they maintained far more ecumenical relations than with Protestant nonconformists in Britain. These matters are examined in Section 2 through an analysis of the significant role played by French Huguenots, such as Elias Neau and Francis Le Jau, in the SPG's early catechising and missionary work amongst enslaved, indigenous, and settler populations in New York and South Carolina.

Persecuted or imprisoned ministers, and boundary crossers, such as missionaries and chaplains, have specific responsibilities and expertise that often require them to operate in transitional spaces with complex entanglements.[19] Pastoral care is both structural (political, economic, parochial) and personal (counselling, administration of rituals, gift-giving), and chaplains and missionaries operate as bridge-builders or spanners between these two levels in various ways. This vulnerable positionality meant that pastors and missionaries faced a range of intersectional and competing accountabilities that could transform their own personal and professional identities. This is evident in the experience of Baxter and other nonconformist ministers after the Restoration, and in the shifting identities and ministerial accountabilities constructed in the letters of the SPG's early missionaries, George Keith, Elias Neau, and Francis Le Jau. Modelling vulnerability in leadership could itself be construed as a form of pastoral care, but one that was less open to administrative representatives for corporations, such as the SPG's Secretary.

---

[16] Sirota, *Christian Monitors*, 223–5. [17] Ibid. 225, 258. [18] Ibid. 259.
[19] Sullivan, *A Ministry of Presence*; Swift, *Hospital Chaplaincy in the Twenty-First Century*.

Pastoral Power and Legacies of Enslavement

Care is an aspect of relationality. Correspondents in both these case studies model and question the power hierarchies involved in epistolary exchange exposing areas of potential abuse. Thinking about pastoral care thus also requires theological and philosophical reflection on pastoral power.[20] It is necessary to recognise the negative dimensions of pastoral care and the legacies of enslavement and colonialism alongside more positive aspects when excavating and reconstructing historical practices of care. There is an imbalance of power in the relationships between pastor/congregant, missionary/audience, doctor and/or chaplain and patient. Michel Foucault's genealogy of pastoral power is useful here. Pastor and sheep are engaged in an affective, reciprocal relationship:

> the Christian pastorate ... establishes a kind of exhaustive, total, and permanent relationship of individual obedience .... [It] is also absolutely innovative in establishing a structure, a technique of, at once, power, investigation, self-examination, and the examination of others, by which a certain secret inner truth of the hidden soul, becomes the element through which the pastor's power is exercised, by which obedience is practiced, by which the relationship of complete obedience is assured.[21]

Foucault argues that this process intensified in the ecclesiastical sphere during the sixteenth century and, as pastoralism enhanced and diversified the technologies available to it, a new modality of government spread beyond the ecclesiastical into the field of political sovereignty.[22]

This intersection between ecclesiastical practice and new methods of government in the development and expansion of pastoral power has important implications for reflecting on practices of pastoral care on the fringes of state authority including, for example, settler zones in North America and the Caribbean, or nonconformist ministers pursuing their vocation in a hostile English nation-state administered parochially. It is significant that Foucault recognises the role of 'pastoral counter-conducts' as well: forms of resistance 'which tend to redistribute, reverse, nullify, and partially or totally discredit pastoral power in the systems of salvation, obedience, and truth'.[23] These border-elements are not external to Christianity, and they seek 'to disrupt the particular alignment of governance' practised by those authorised to provide pastoral care. Such forms of resistance include asceticism (which challenges the emphasis on obedience to the other by prioritising the self), community formation, the cultivation of mysticism (which disrupts the pastorate's political

---

[20] See Dillen, ed., *Soft Shepherd or Almighty Pastor?*
[21] Foucault, *Security, Terror, Population*, 183.   [22] Ibid. 227–83.   [23] Ibid. 204.

mobilisation of truth through circumventing examination), a return to scripture, and embracing eschatology.[24]

Foucault's historical account of the development of pastoral power within the Western Christian tradition has limitations, but his analysis of the configurations of power operating within specific Protestant communities, and the opportunities border-elements offer for counter-conduct,[25] enable an assessment of the intersections between knowledge, power, and care in early modern correspondence archives. The utility of pastoral power as a concept lies in its capacity to render visible the potential abuses that pastoral care as a seemingly benign term can inadvertently obscure. Foucault's genealogy of pastoral power calibrates a simplistic win/lose model of exchange where there is a finite amount of power and if one person 'loses' power then another must 'gain' some allowing for a more attenuated account of how benevolence and violence intersect when giving and receiving pastoral care: '[T]he pastor, according to Foucault, has a hermeneutical role of hearing and interpreting the confession such that they can guide the individual toward self-understanding'.[26] Such intimate and implicitly reciprocal exchanges are essential to creating and reinscribing but also potentially disrupting the minister's authority. This interpersonal dynamic is not circumvented when thinking about dialogical exchanges via letter, though its textual inscription through the medium of correspondence shapes it in particular ways. The authority of the pastor, like that of the physician, is established by the fact that they each hold knowledges and sets of professional expertise.[27] Such expertise was developed and distributed across the British Atlantic through the SPG's structure as an incorporated company: expertise was shared through epistolary exchanges that also demonstrated the importance, and frequent absence, of the Anglican church's episcopal authority beyond England. Paperwork, with letters as the core genre, remains key here.

The interpersonal dynamics both individual and social involved in recuperating a genealogy of pastoral care in early modern religious communities is enriched by an interdisciplinary approach, particularly when dealing with the British Atlantic in the late-seventeenth and early-eighteenth centuries. Willie James Jennings's theological analysis of the historical intersections between European colonisation, the emergence of global Christian missions, and the development of theories of race recalibrates Foucault's account of pastoral power, unpicking the implications of intersectionality when reflecting on

---

[24] Ibid. 204–15; Golder, 'Foucault', 174.

[25] Foucault notes that 'these counter-conducts are clearly not absolutely external to Christianity, but are actually border-elements, if you like, which have been continually re-utilized, re-implanted, and taken up again in one or another direction'. *Security, Terror, Population*, 214–5.

[26] Mayes, 'Pastoral Power', 488.   [27] Ibid. 489.

pastoral caregiving through letters not only in terms of clergy/laity, male/female binaries but also in terms of black/white and enslaved/free. The SPG archive makes two things clear: recuperation of practices of pastoral care in the early modern British Atlantic must also consider the engagement of British Protestants in transatlantic slavery, commerce, and exchange; any act of pastoral caregiving is also an act of pastoral power. This power can be benevolent, violent, or any spectrum of possibilities between and in combination. However, the SPG's archive documents experiments in providing pastoral care resourced by enslaved people as well as to enslaved people. The intimate complexities of the religious, social, political, and economic entanglements that these experiments in pastoral care necessitated were profoundly deforming and impacted those exploited in traumatic ways. The challenge then is to produce an account of pastoral care that also reckons with this legacy of enslavement: 'A Christianity born of such realities but historically formed to resist them has yielded a form of religious life that thwarts its deepest instincts of intimacy . . .. [T]he intimacy that marks Christian history is a painful one, in which the joining often meant oppression, violence, and death, if not of bodies then most certainly of ways of life, forms of language, and visions of the world.'[28]

Pastoral caregiving as a component of Christian mission and pedagogy strengthened the reach and power of transatlantic colonial endeavours. Jennings notes that attempts

> to teach and thereby create orthodoxy even in those [designated] the most ignorant flesh, black Africans, produced a reductive theological vision in which the world's people become perpetual students, even where and when faith is formed. What will grow out of this horrid colonial arrangement is a form of imperialism far more flexible, subtle, and virulent than could be explained by appeals to cultural difference or ethnic chauvinism. This imperialist form drew life from Christianity's lifeblood, from its missionary mandate and its mission reflexes. It was therefore poised to follow its currents all along its geographic length and its nationalist breadth, profoundly marking its body.[29]

Jennings argues that replacing theology with pedagogy allowed evaluation to become a constant operation of the modality of knowledge/power: 'Through that modality, the native subject was formed into a deficient barbarian in need of continuous external and internal self-examination and evaluation. How well or how poorly the evaluations are done stands inside this human subject-generating discursive formation.'[30]

---

[28] Jennings, *The Christian Imagination*, 9. See also Johnson, *Wicked Flesh*.
[29] Jennings, *The Christian Imagination*, 112.   [30] Ibid. 106.

This distorting and theologically inflected process of subject-formation was materially reproduced within transatlantic genealogies of pastoral care such as those evidenced and inscribed by the archives that inform the two case studies examined here. Evaluation was an essential aspect of the roles of missionaries, pastors, and chaplains: embodied in intellectuals and 'vivified in the presence of subordinate natives', it becomes the 'means through which Christian tradition must be articulated in the New World'; the process of 'forming productive workers ... merged with ... forming theological subjects'. Pastoral power is thus dispersed 'through a network of relations that include the priest, his action ... his response to native actions, and his activity in relation to the actions of others upon native bodies'.[31] An early letter sent by the French Huguenot, Elias Neau, to the SPG's Treasurer, John Hodges, on 10 July 1703, brings the material logistics that pastoral care presented into stark relief. Neau suggests that rather than ministering to Native Americans, it would be more appropriate for the SPG to focus on the conversion of enslaved people in New York 'of whom \there is no manner of/ Care taken'. The letter outlines the qualities required of the person selected for this type of work, demonstrating how missionary observation could shape and inform the SPG's decision-making and evaluation of appropriate candidates for service in London. Neau also notes that for the provision of pastoral care to be enforceable in an economy dependent on plantation slavery, legal protection and coercion is required to reassure owners of enslaved people that baptism did not entail manumission: spiritual freedom could not liberate from material bondage.[32]

Theorisations of care entangle technologies and definitions of 'the human'. Christopher Codrington's bequest is a cogent example of how the affective, economic, pastoral, medical, and imperial were entwined in order to facilitate the SPG's pastoral caregiving on a global scale. How appropriate objects of care were defined (or excluded) in the early modern British Atlantic, and the ways this shaped systemic structures created to resource and provide care, has affinities with current efforts to interrogate care, both as a concept,[33] and as a socio-political challenge.[34] This is sharply focalised through posthumanism. The etymology of 'robot' is connected to slave labour, and in the present, 'robotic (and non-human animal) care is poised to step into the minoritized breach of contemporary care work'. Interrogated by dystopian fiction, 'the gendered and racialized affective economies ... that depend on the emotional and physical labour of marginalized workers',[35] are made manifest. Imagination's

---

[31] Ibid. 107.   [32] SPG 13 28–9.
[33] Kittay, 'The Ethics of Care'; Sloane, *Vulnerability and Care*; Tronto, 'An Ethic of Care'.
[34] Bunting, *Labours of Love*; Dowling, *The Care Crisis*.
[35] DeFalco, 'Towards a Theory of Posthuman Care'.

affordances and its limits, especially communal and temporal configurations, are critical to understanding, expanding, and constraining what it means to provide and receive care. John Hearne depicts such a moment in his novel, *The Sure Salvation*, when the captain of an English ship becalmed in the Atlantic takes pleasure in writing an entry in the logbook: 'It was not often at sea that [Hogarth] could experience the dutiful pleasure of fashioning letters as he had been taught . . . . Now, in this calm, the deck steady as the floor of a room, his fist returned effortlessly to its first lessons . . . he closed his log on the lines that read *Noon, May 17, 1860 – Lat 1° 14' S, Long 32° 16' W. No distance. Calm continues. Full sails set. Cargo in prime condition because of our special care.*' This '*Cargo*' consisted of 'four hundred and seventy-five bodies he had discriminately culled from along the coast from the Congo to Angola'. As Hazel V. Carby concludes:

> Hogarth's pleasure in his accomplished hand denied the hand that traded in human flesh, revealing the depths of its inhumanity with each letter of '*Cargo in prime condition because of our special care.*'
>
> Acts of gracious writing that account for empire are evidence of the bottomless depths of unacknowledged violence and brutality embodied in British character and values across the colonial and imperial landscape.[36]

This Element's account of pastoral care needs to be sufficiently capacious to encompass the wide range of spiritual and material experiences of entangled communities from the two case studies examined. Developing such a concept and genealogy of pastoral care could flatten incommensurate realities through affinities that prove spurious. The freighted legacies shaping the creation of the archives considered mean that it is necessary to formulate a vocabulary for the administration and practice of pastoral caregiving, as it developed and can be traced in these early letters, that incorporates as far as possible the contribution and experience of enslaved peoples, as well as Europeans of various nationalities and Christian beliefs, and Native Americans. This keeps the key question of how pastoral caregiving was materially resourced and at what cost central to the analysis of developing spiritual practices, literary forms, and administrative structures. Such entanglements are global as well as local, underwritten by theological as well as colonial imperatives that do not always work well together. A robust account of pastoral care informed by a genealogy of pastoral power enables a richer historical account of these entanglements and allows nonconformist correspondence archives such as Baxter's to be reframed within a transatlantic context, including an assessment of how Baxter's casuistical methods shape his epistolary caregiving.

---

[36] Carby, *Imperial Intimacies*, 230–1. The quotation from Hearne's novel is also taken from Carby.

Letters of Pastoral Care

Letters were the material and technological mechanism that facilitated how pastoral care was imagined and provided in the zones of experimentation and entanglement examined here. Their production and transportation were shaped by, and in turn helped to form, political, commercial, and educational structures within and outside the state church and nonconformist institutions. Reliable postal and shipping networks enabling communication via letter were crucial to the success of spiritual and commercial ventures across the British Atlantic in the early modern period. This can be evidenced through the initial achievements of the sole slave trader, Humphry Morice, at the expense of the Royal African Company in the early decades of the eighteenth century. However, 'the amount of time it took Company letters to travel from Africa to London improved at only an extremely slow rate throughout the first half of the eighteenth century, speeding up modestly after 1750'.[37] Nonetheless, developments in new over-ground postal routes and services in Britain, the Caribbean, and North America, a significant increase in the amount of traffic crossing the Atlantic, as well as innovations in setting up regular services for the exchange of letters, papers, and packages meant that the 'flow of political, business, or personal correspondence quickened even if most travel times remained the same'.[38] These developments shaped how individuals and corporations imagined and participated in transatlantic communication. They also created expectations for regular reporting, reciprocal exchange, and accountability that could place increasing administrative burdens on literate missionaries, clergy, and schoolteachers engaged in pastoral care. This was seen by some as a benefit, facilitating the receiving as well as giving of pastoral care through letters by those working in remote locations on the fringes of empire.

There is an expanding literature on the material letter,[39] institutional archives and how they shape our understanding of historical documents,[40] and the religious republic of letters,[41] which is integral to the critical, historical, and theological ways in which my analysis of epistolary caregiving is framed. Letters of pastoral care have a distinct history and can be identified as an epistolary subgenre that encodes textual caregiving in a particular literary form. A significant portion of the New Testament, and some parts of the Old Testament, for example, the prophet Jeremiah's letter to the Jewish exiles in

---

[37] Mitchell, *The Prince of Slavers*, 219.
[38] Steele, *The English Atlantic, 1675–1740*, 114. See also 113–31, 168–88.
[39] Daybell, *The Material Letter in Early Modern England*.
[40] Bross, *Future History*; Peters, Walsham, & Corens, eds., *Archives and Information*.
[41] Furey, *Erasmus, Contarini, and the Religious Republic of Letters*; Hardy, *Criticism and Confession*.

Babylon,[42] were written and preserved in epistolary form, offering pastoral care to exiled communities and missionary-founded churches across the Roman empire. The genre of the pastoral letter has a lengthy history and, through its incorporation in the Christian scriptures, has exercised a significant influence as a form and model for public engagement. Pastoral theology can be understood as public theology when an idea 'contributes to the transformation of public human conditions, engaging itself in public debates over issues such as family, public health, and welfare policies'.[43] Letters provide important evidence of theological reflection and practice in process and under pressure, as correspondents engage reflexively with the conundrums and challenges created by persecution, isolation, cultural estrangement, and geographical distance. The importance of biblical exemplars as models of pastoral care provision through letters can be seen in the way early modern Protestants such as Samuel Rutherford, Joseph Alleine, and John Bunyan, drew overtly on the biblical epistles as templates to authorise their own literary caregiving practices.[44]

Pastoral letters are a unique textual, and therefore material (due to their reliance on paper manufacture, availability, and developing infrastructures of communication across the early modern British Atlantic) technology that enable (as an affordance) the provision of literary caregiving across space and time. While technology is often construed as presentist, or primarily future-orientated, writing is a powerful skill (*techne*) that has been deployed in constructive and coercive terms by humans for millennia.[45] As epistolary documents that inscribe spiritual, emotional, political, and physical power and affect, on paper, that can be exchanged, intercepted, interpreted, censored, edited, treasured, and destroyed, pastoral letters as a material technology were essential to the construction of experimental, innovative, and coercive networks of literary caregiving across the early modern British Atlantic. This material infrastructure of paperwork, mechanisms for transport across land and sea, and access to literacy (as writers and readers) also facilitated the creation of a metaphorical discursive space that was crucial to how Baxter, the SPG, missionaries, catechists, pastors, and their congregants imagined and enacted the provision, receipt, coercion, and exchange of pastoral care across political, geographical, cultural, and ecclesiological boundaries.

Epistolary care involved getting the recipient of a pastoral letter to write back and thus required at least two active participants; a third person sometimes acted as a broker soliciting care on behalf of another individual/group expanding the

---

[42] Jeremiah, 29:1–32.   [43] Park, 'An Evolving History', 27.
[44] Davies, 'Spirit in the Letters'; Harris, "Heroick Virtue"; Searle & Vine, "We Have Sick Souls When God's Physic Works Not".
[45] Fleming, *Cultural Graphology*; Ballantyne & Patterson, eds., *Indigenous Textual Cultures*.

reach of literary caregiving further still. Gary Schneider notes that the unique conventions of the letter form can result in specific rhetorical outcomes. Schneider focuses on print correspondence, but the performative dimension of pastoral care provided through letters means that his taxonomy of the genre is useful when reflecting on how epistolary care operates in literary terms. These features include the assumption that letters allow access into one's inner thoughts; they possess documentary and transmissive properties and tie two or more people together in a social bond; letter exchange involves reciprocity; letters embed language in textual form, and specifically in seventeenth-century England, they informed news culture.[46]

Letters were crucial to intersubjective communication across the early modern British Atlantic, and fictive personas were an important aspect of how correspondence networks and remote communication were imagined, created, and actualised over long distances and diverse cultural geographies. As a communication technology, letters encode affect and facilitate dialogical exchange: this is a significant aspect of their affordance as a literary genre. Clare Brant has analysed the character types adopted by letter writers in eighteenth-century Britain, including parents, lovers, criminals, citizens, travellers, historians, and Christians.[47] Extending this typology further to consider the fictive persona of incorporated companies such as the SPG enriches our understanding of epistolary culture in the period, and makes evident how processes of writing, imagining, and identity formation, both individual and corporate, intersect to create new communities shaped by structures of pastoral care and power across the British Atlantic.

Soliciting, giving, and receiving pastoral care through letters introduces questions of reciprocity and vulnerability. These are further inflected by the status, class, and gender of sender and recipient, the relationship between metropole and periphery, and whether an individual or group's religious identity has been proscribed by the state. Letters were the only textual communication technology available to early modern women and men who were separated due to distance, persecution, or other reasons. Letter-writing was an essential activity for literate individuals in the early modern British Atlantic, but it also rendered one vulnerable: to censorship; exposure; no response, a missing response, an aggressive response; or to unauthorised publication by the recipient. Letters were thus necessary to the provision of remote pastoral care in this period, but the contingent factors that shaped the writing, sending, and receipt of correspondence rendered epistolary care distinct from pastoral care administered in other ways.

---

[46] Schneider, *Print Letters in Seventeenth-Century England*, 6–9.
[47] Brant, *Eighteenth-Century Letters*.

These specific features of the letter include its implicit elicitation of a response from its recipient; its capacity to travel long distances; its ability to act as a cover for, or index to, accompanying objects such as books, gifts, provisions, or indeed the bearer themselves; its capacity to bestow credit; and its prosthetic inscription, enactment, and distortion of the communion of saints as the body of Christ.

1 Contentious Caregiving in a Divided State

This section examines the politics of pastoral caregiving within the context of a divided English state in the mid-to-late-seventeenth century. The use of letters as a textual technology for soliciting, dispensing, and receiving pastoral care is assessed through an analysis of Richard Baxter's epistolary ecumenism, treatment of melancholy, and the limits of each in the late 1650s. I then examine the methodological porosity between occasional meditation and natural philosophy; these inform Baxter's holistic pastoral care provision through letters and demonstrate his distinctive engagement in the republic of letters as it is inflected by a transtemporal theological concept of the communion of saints that he shared with many of his correspondents. Restoration censorship of nonconformity generated specific casuistical problems for Baxter and the section concludes with a consideration of how these shaped epistolary accounts of his own experience, and his response to requests for guidance by other pastoral caregivers through letters.

One of the most prolific writers in seventeenth-century England, Richard Baxter has always been difficult to label:

> his willingness to associate with men of all parties and his doctrinal eclecticism, is a trait born of his open-mindedness. In him an absolute Christian commitment, which we recognize as Puritan, leads not to any narrowing of his sympathies, but to a responsiveness to the best in all men's thinking and practice, and a passionate desire that by the development of all their faculties men may grow as moral and spiritual beings.[48]

Baxter was an effective pastor and casuist and his influence extended across the early modern Protestant British Atlantic. His reputation was based on his successful Interregnum ministry in Kidderminster, which was profiled through his publications: 'It was here that he developed his distinctive pastoral theology and the practice of one-to-one instruction and conversation with every parish member: decidedly not a gathered church model of the testifying elect but an open invitation to all residents in the parish, however compromised or anxious, to share in Christian community.'[49]

---

[48] Keeble, *Richard Baxter*, 47.　　[49] Keeble, 'The Reformed Pastor', 140.

Many of Baxter's publications became serial bestsellers: *The Saints' Everlasting Rest* (1650), which grew out of sermons preached to his congregation and was written up during a period of sickness; *Gildas Salvianus: The Reformed Pastor* (1656), drawing on Baxter's professional experience as a preacher and catechist (this volume has never been out of print); and *A Christian Directory* (1673), compressing his practical divinity and casuistry into a single reference work over one-million words in length targeted at pastors and families. Baxter's books, written in a direct, colloquial style, led many of his readers, including apprentices, ministers, gentlewomen, aristocrats, missionaries, and academics to respond with letters seeking advice, asking for comfort, taking issue with his theology, and requesting his political support or medical expertise. The increased liberty granted by the Commonwealth and Protectorate facilitated the creation of more flexible ecclesial structures allowing heterodox groups to participate in corporate worship. However, the Restoration precipitated a legislative pro-gramme that established religious nonconformists as a significant minority. These newly proscribed communities created mechanisms through which to nourish and sustain their personal and corporate spirituality, identities, and doctrinal convictions. Letters were integral to this community sustenance and instruction; both geographical and temporal distance shaped the experience of pastoral care solicited, given, and received in such a way.

The Politics of Pastoral Care

Baxter used letters, both in manuscript and print, to provide pastoral care in an epistolary form largely outside the English state's ecclesial structures, rendering him frequently vulnerable to censorship, imprisonment, or other forms of persecution for his principled leadership of nonconformity. The giving and receiving of care through letters involved negotiating power hierarchies, the encoding of affect, and balancing sometimes incommensurate personal and corporate priorities; in some respects, the privations Baxter faced may have restricted how pastoral caregiving was imagined. Care is an aspect of relation-ality and power hierarchies are inevitable. Baxter, and his diverse correspond-ents, model and assess how these hierarchies could be inhabited and where there is potential for abuse. Central to all epistolary care was getting the recipient of a pastoral letter to write back.

Caregiving is inherently political – in terms of identifying who is worthy of care, how caregiving within the body politic is resourced, how caregivers are themselves cared for, and the importance of attending to the spiritual as well as material aspects of care in a situation of heightened mortality and fear. This meant that the provision of pastoral care was particularly contentious in a society as religiously and politically divided as seventeenth-century England. Some of these tensions are interrogated by Baxter in *The cure of Church-divisions: or, Directions for weak Christians, to keep them from being Dividers, or Troublers of the Church* (1670).

> How long Lord, must thy Church and Cause, be in the hands of unexperienced furious fools, who know not what Holiness or Healing is, but think that victory over mens Bodies, must be the cure of their Souls, and that hurting them is the way to win their Love! or that a Church is constituted of *Bodies* alone while *Souls* are absent, or no parts! who will make themselves the Rulers of thy Flock in despite of thee and of thy Cause and Servants, without thy call or approbation, and think that the work of a Soldier, is the work of a *Father* and a *Physician*! whose cures are all by amputation; and whose piety consisteth in flying from each other, and esteeming and using their Brethren as their foes . . . . They that think that if they could get and keep the upper ground, and have Dissenters bodies and estates at their will, they would soon settle the Church in Unity and Concord, do tell all the world, how ignorant they are of the nature of Christianity.[50]

Baxter here highlights intersections between the material and spiritual. As a reluctant nonconformist excluded from the state church, he recognises how religious authorities police conformity under the guise of pastoral care; it becomes a central mechanism of political and ecclesial governance. Arguments of the type that Baxter models and publishes in *The cure of Church-divisions* can be understood as a form of caregiving, enacted dialogically, leading in ideal circumstances to a point of mutual consent. For Baxter, however, this dimension of epistolary care was gendered, and he addressed women and men differently when dealing with doctrinal disputes. The fact that this book was found in the library of the conformist, Lady Anne Clifford, suggests that Baxter's print polemics, aimed at comprehension for nonconformists within the national church, were not entirely without hope of fulfilment: 'Clifford was interested in reading what Baxter had to say in 1670. Perhaps it was the ecumenical message of the book that attracted her.'[51]

There were specific historical conditions that made Baxter's role as a provider of pastoral care particularly contentious: 'The consequence of an unprecedentedly severe form of Anglican aggression was an unprecedentedly aggressive form of moderate puritanism.'[52] Baxter was a nonconformist due to 'a principled refusal to consent to a national church founded on prescriptions intended to be exclusive and to coerce consciences into uniformity'.[53]

[50] Baxter, *Cure of Church Divisions*, B2v-4r.
[51] Malay, 'Reassessing Anne Clifford's Books', 14.   [52] Winship, 'Defining Puritanism', 705.
[53] Keeble, 'The Reformed Pastor', 139.

N. H. Keeble argues that the shift in vocation that the 1662 Act of Uniformity required worked against Baxter's genius. By 1689 'the sacrifice of thirty years of pastoral care in the service of the ideal of a comprehensive church had come to nothing'.[54] This gap between vocation and practical opportunities for service continued to energise Baxter's creative and prolific use of the epistolary genre. His letter-writing activity following the Restoration represents a similar commitment to pastoral care from the grassroots up to that he sought to achieve through his ministry at Kidderminster and via the Worcestershire Association during the Interregnum.[55]

There is also a strong corporeal dimension to Baxter's critique of the Church of England's pastoral care that indicts the ecclesiastical authorities precisely for their lack of spiritual discernment in focusing on the material rather than the spiritual: 'who know not what Holiness or Healing is, but think that victory over mens Bodies, must be the cure of their Souls'. Instead of modelling their vocation on God as father and physician, they mistakenly adopt the military solution of soldiers and consider a violent amputation as the only appropriate form of cure.[56] Baxter attempts to reinscribe himself and his fellow nonconformists into this national ecclesial space not as outcasts whose estates are ripe for plunder, but as brethren who are being misidentified as enemies. This is print polemic designed to reshape public discussion about the administration of pastoral care in a contentious state context. Unsurprisingly, Baxter had difficulty publishing it.[57]

Epistolary Ecumenism, Melancholy, and Pastoral Vocation in the late 1650s

Practices of pastoral care amongst godly communities in mid-seventeenth-century England had to adapt to a series of crises including state church disestablishment, persecution, and civil war; '[a]n enduring relationship between pastor and people ... became of paramount importance for the godly programme of parish reformation'.[58] Ecclesial experiments, such as those practised by credobaptists, unmoored the idea of community from the physical territory of the parish creating a '"virtual" ideological identity for the godly that could be spread through nodes of contact'.[59] The exchange of letters providing pastoral care established and nourished such nodes of contact and can be interpreted as a form of literary

---

[54] Ibid. 149, 151.

[55] Joel Halcomb's work provides a corrective to the tendency to over-emphasise Baxter's importance in the association movement at a national level. Halcomb, 'The Association Movement'.

[56] Baxter, *The Cure of Church Divisions*, B2v-4r.

[57] Keeble et al. eds., *Reliquiae Baxterianae*, V, 276–7.

[58] Vernon, 'Godly Pastors and their Congregations', 48.

[59] Lynch, "Letting a Room in a London-House", 64.

caregiving; they show the key role played by words in godly communities during periods of trauma and change.[60] Evidencing the dialogical ways in which pastoral care functioned within a broad puritan literary tradition in Interregnum England, these letters operationalised the communion of saints, and enabled the brief flourishing of a more inclusive vision of church reformation.

Tim Cooper explores how discourse shapes social formation and group boundaries and what this means for defining Baxter's relationship with different ecclesiological models, particularly Congregationalism, in England in the late 1650s. Cooper traces how Baxter reframes his own position on church polity depending on his specific interlocutor or audience. This is an obvious point, but it highlights something worth noting when reading letters of pastoral care: they are fashioned in dialogue with the specific needs and concerns of the person or people to whom they are addressed. Cooper uses an epistolary exchange between Baxter and one of his Kidderminster parishioners, Edward Burton, as an example, and the subject is whether Baxter's Kidderminster congregation is a gathered church or not. This letter does not reveal Baxter at his most irenic; he responds irately to Burton's charges. But the exchange does expose the power dynamics inherent within relationships of pastoral care and the contentious nature of ecclesial structures of caregiving and oversight within parish church ministry in the late Interregnum.[61] These tensions only became more pronounced after the Restoration, but Baxter's 1658 correspondence with Burton shows that even when Baxter was able freely to fulfil his role as a minister within the parish of Kidderminster, the collapse of consensus about the structure of the national church meant that parishioners could actively challenge the ecclesiological policy and practice of the incumbent pastor, and that letter-writing was an important strand of pastoral care and oversight alongside preaching, home visits, and catechising. It is possible to consider Burton's pub conversations and opposition to aspects of Baxter's exercise of pastoral power in Kidderminster as a type of Foucauldian counter-conduct or form of resistance within the parish. Burton was 'apparently accused of being 'a Cavileere or Malignant, An Episcopall man' and 'the great Enemie' to Baxter and his church.[62] This makes the political dimensions of Interregnum ecclesiology, and its interconnections with pastoral caregiving at the local level, evident, even if, as Cooper argues, Baxter's own relationship with Congregationalism was more attenuated than this letter indicates.

---

[60] The term 'literary caregiving' is used by Sara Haslam in her analysis of reading and the provision of care during the First World War. Haslam, 'Reading, Trauma and Literary Caregiving'. It has been developed further by Searle & Vine, "We Have Sick Souls When God's Physic Works Not". On the emergence of bibliotherapy, see Miller, 'Medicines of the Soul'.

[61] Cooper, 'Polity and Peacemaking', 200–21.   [62] Ibid. 200.

Provision of pastoral care through letters generally focuses spiritual attention on the one rather than the many, and it is necessary to recognise that such exchanges have at least two dimensions and often more. Foucault's genealogy of pastoral power allows us to account both for the subtleties in how pastoral care constructs the subject in relation to authority (whether priest or physician) and the opportunities afforded to subjects by the medium of the letter to respond freely in ways that transform the dynamics of the exchange when receiving pastoral care. Ann Hughes's analysis of the devotional writings and practice of the Derbyshire gentlewoman, Katherine Gell, and her household, make the specific affordances of the letter as a genre in this context clear. Writing was an essential aspect of Gell's devotional life and is evidenced in a range of genres including letters, recipe books, poetry, journals, and sermon notes. Hughes suggests that one way in which Gell may have responded to the epistolary advice of Baxter, and the Presbyterian minister, Robert Porter, was in moderating her diary or journal writing, and focusing on sermon notes: 'Reflection and self-examination were necessary but could become self-indulgent and self-defeating. Sermon note-taking, on the other hand, was a strenuous, intellectual activity that might put individual struggles in a broader, more manageable and externalised context'.[63]

Just as writing sermon notes involves the auditor reflecting on and appropriating ideas in an internal dialogue with the preacher, so letter-writing encourages a movement beyond the self, particularly if one is seeking pastoral care from a recognised authority. Gell wrote to Baxter after reading his *Saints' Rest* – while deeply influential, it was also critiqued by some for its strenuous programme of heavenly meditation; a pastorally dangerous burden for sensitive consciences.[64] Baxter was aware of this and sought to ameliorate the impact in his letters of pastoral care to Gell. However, Gell did not appreciate being told to focus on the care and management of her household and did not always accept the diagnosis of her spiritual and physical health provided by Baxter. She owns her melancholic disposition but argued that her sorrows cannot be wholly explained by that and emerge instead from 'spiritual wants'. The dialogical exchange inherent to pastoral care requested and provided through letters created space for Gell to assess and sometimes disagree with the conclusions drawn by the clerical epistolary counsellors she had selected herself. Here gender and professional authority are offset by Gell's superior social status, and an independent judgement developed through reading, writing, and

---

[63] Hughes, "A Soul Preaching to Itself", 66–9.

[64] Ibid. Porter touches on this in his correspondence with Gell. It is also raised by Giles Firmin in publication and correspondence with Baxter. See, for example, Baxter's response on 1 October 1670. Keeble & Nuttall, *Calendar*, Vol. 2, 99.

reflection. Elite women often acted as patrons to puritan clergy who were both clients and counsellors. Gell informed Baxter that by 'a way contrary to all advise (viz) reading I found Mr Gurnalls *Christian Armour* did soe revive me and refresh my spirits that it set me much above any such things as used to discompose me'.[65]

Andrew McKendry has examined how Baxter's apparent inclusiveness and respect for human diversity incorporated assumptions about individual capability that could be coercive, cruel, and exclusionary: melancholy is the intractable condition that exposes the systemic inadequacies of Baxter's logic of rehabilitation. This partial deconstruction of Baxter as an irenic, well-informed counsellor, capable of providing a distinctive blend of pastoral and medical advice is an important corrective to earlier scholarly assessments. The high stakes involved in providing pastoral care through printed books and letters can be seen in an instance where Baxter's advice on dealing with melancholy was explicitly cited in a suicide note.[66] Melancholics show the limits of 'a system of justice premised on capability . . . as well as what collateral damage its procedures and practices might cause'.[67] Baxter's reader is constructed 'as presumptively able-bodied', but Baxter confronted a backlash for 'exalting capability and self-determination' as elements of the 'common reader' and this shows 'how historically contingent [his] imagined reader is'.[68] The pastoral letter as a genre and technology requires us to consider further the shifting dynamics of power between writer and reader within the context of reciprocal epistolary exchange. Personal manuscript letters of pastoral care invite the reader to be imagined as a particular person, such as Katherine Gell, or Edward Burton, and this differs from the imagined 'common reader' of a published work aimed at a diverse audience. The dialogical exchange inherent to the genre also matters. Though Baxter defines Gell as melancholic, and shapes his pastoral advice based on that assumption, she remains recalcitrant; Gell's reply demonstrates that she is not prepared to passively accept his combined diagnosis and proffered solution.

Baxter was pragmatic in his writing practices: he knew that certain things could only be achieved through publishing for a broad audience, and he was also aware of the epistolary protocols governing the exchange of personal correspondence. His decision, at times, to print letters exchanged in manuscript as part of his published writings indicates that he viewed this boundary as porous: necessity always outweighed literary decorum. However, manuscript letters also offered Baxter the opportunity to expand his provision of personalised

---

[65] Hughes, "A Soul Preaching to Itself", 67.   [66] McKendry, *Disavowing Disability*, 62–3.
[67] Ibid. 5.   [68] Ibid. 30.

pastoral care, particularly in relation to women, as it excluded the potentialities of sexual transgression that meeting with them one-on-one as part of his parish duties opened up.[69] Such letters also foreground the personal dimension, which was deeply significant to Baxter, in part because it facilitated a more powerful, effective, and intimate application of pastoral care to the needs of the individual with whom he is corresponding. Writing pastoral letters allowed Baxter to make himself available for care and support without feeling so imperative a necessity to inscribe disciplinary correctness and defend theological boundaries as he did when writing with a view to publication, but this remains a distinction of degree rather than kind.

Numerous women approached Baxter for pastoral advice through letters. Another such was Barbara Lambe. With her husband, Thomas, a leather merchant, and his associate, William Allen, she played a significant role in leading a group to break away from the congregation of the Independent minister, John Goodwin, in the early 1650s, to form a separate church defined by its commitment to credobaptism. The original twenty or so members had increased to one hundred or more by 12 August 1658, when Barbara decided to write to Baxter. Despite his role as co-founder and leader of this new congregation, Thomas was increasingly uncertain about his decision to restrict church communion on the grounds of baptism, and Barbara was concerned for Thomas's mental and spiritual health.[70] It is not possible fully to reconstruct the role that Barbara may have played in creating a sizeable London congregation identifiable by its distinctive beliefs about baptism, but Baxter describes her as 'an extraordinary intelligent woman' in his memoir and her initiative in contacting him via letter, without informing her husband, demonstrates her resourcefulness.[71] The resulting correspondence shows the agency women could exercise within gathered congregations, Barbara's theological acumen, and the qualified respect accorded to her by male leaders. In her second letter to Baxter, she suggests he should write to Allen, but asks that he not mention 'any knowlige' of her, 'for [Allen] hath ben apt to sermise that I have ocasioned my husbands late thoughts which god knowes I did not in the least at first'.[72]

Barbara played a significant role navigating congregational and doctrinal politics in a turbulent historical moment. Her motivation was twofold: to ensure her husband's well-being through sourcing appropriate pastoral care and to build a wider coalition of believers and churches united despite varying beliefs

---

[69] Baxter, *Gildas Salvianus*, 426–7.

[70] For fuller discussion of the context see Bingham, 'English Radical Religion'; Coffey, *John Goodwin*; Ha, 'Freedom of Association'; More, 'Congregationalism and the Social Order'.

[71] Cited in Keeble et al., eds., *Reliquiae Baxterianae*, Vol. 3, 186.

[72] Keeble & Nuttall, *Calendar*, Vol. 1, 341.

about baptism. These goals were achieved through letters as a material technology that allowed for both communication and network formation. Her correspondence requires a reappraisal of the connections between the emergence of credobaptism as a communal church practice in England, its implications for the constitution of local churches, and how pastoral care was provided in these contexts. Barbara was a significant actor in the 1650s ecclesiological debates about credobaptism, but she also helped to dissolve a prominent credobaptist congregation. Barbara's opening letter to Baxter demonstrates the challenge of separating her role in these church activities from her husband's, which is probably a calculated choice on her part: 'The Case is mine only, as it is the Case of one who is my self in the dear Relation of a Husband.'[73] Her letters reveal the multiple valences of credobaptism as a doctrine, practice, and congregational marker. Barbara embraced the opportunity to engage with intellectual and theological experiments that shaped ecclesiological identities and her correspondence with Baxter shows how affect, and hierarchies of gender and authority were encoded in epistolary form; letters enabled the careful negotiation of personal and corporate priorities for pastoral care in a highly volatile political context.

Barbara's decision to write to Baxter about her husband's situation, though she had never met him, demonstrates pastoral acumen; she builds a persuasive rhetorical case as to why he should assist her by affectively invoking the communion of saints.

> Perhaps my Boldness may seem much in this Address to one unknown by Face; but want of that is no sufficient Plea to restrain me, knowing it's no Impediment to the Communion of Saints. These lines are writ out of much Affliction of Heart, and in many Tears which have run over at the Throne of Grace many a time about the Case presented. The Reason of my Address to you, rather than any other, is because of some Converse I have had with your Writings.[74]

The direct conversational style of Baxter's publications persuaded Barbara that he would be willing to engage in an epistolary exchange. She narrates the history of the congregation where her husband is an elder, and then notes that for nine months his disrelish of those who unchurch all besides themselves has prompted him 'to consider the Grounds of separating upon the account of Baptism'.[75] His reading of works by Baxter, Thomas Goodwin, and Nathaniel Homes has 'begot in him not only a Sight of Weakness in his Grounds about Separating, but weakened his Confidence as to the opposing of Infant Baptism'.[76] '[B]eing free and open Hearted', Thomas shared these views with

---

[73] Keeble et al., eds., *Reliquiae Baxterianae*, Vol. 3, 188.   [74] Ibid.   [75] Ibid. 189.   [76] Ibid.

some 'who being rigid about Separation, still persuaded him these new Thoughts were Satan's Temptations'.[77] Barbara outlines Thomas's fears at great length, including his anxiety that carnal motivations to make better marriages for his daughters (who, as she notes, are only ten and eleven years old at this point), might be prompting him to reject 'strait Principles' of separation, concluding this 'hath filled *his Soul with great distress, which I declare to you as a spiritual Physician, that you may know the whole Case'*.[78] Barbara invokes the common medical analogy of the pastor as a physician of the soul, providing a comprehensive account of Thomas's fears of apostasy, melancholy, and the offence and disturbance he is causing to 'the People to whom he is Elder'.[79]

Barbara does not leave the epistolary diagnosis of her husband's spiritual condition entirely to Baxter. She combines self-deprecation with shrewdness when persuading him to provide the pastoral care her husband needs following the impact that his shifting views about baptism have had on his own health and on the members of his gathered congregation: 'Now, dear Sir, I hope you understand my Scriblings, the end of all is to intreat your help as one that Christ hath set in his Church for the edifying and establishing of his Members; judging you faithful, and one of a Thousand in experience ....'[80] This is followed by six pointed queries, which effectively diagnose her husband's case, based on the narrative account she has provided in the letter, covering the cause of temptation, the reason for distress of spirit, the appropriate relationship with Goodwin's congregation, his duty as a minister to the congregation of the re-baptised he has gathered, the limits of communion, and whether 'it be his present Work to study to be setled in a full Persuasion one way or other about Baptism'.[81]

Barbara concludes: 'shall I have so much Grace in your Sight, as to have your distinct Answer to these Particulars; truly, it will be Service to Jesus Christ'.[82] Her decision to write to Baxter has created difficulties, so she requests his secrecy, asking that any reply be enclosed in a cover addressed to her son-in-law, as 'were it known, it might occasion me some *farther Tryals'*.[83] This is accompanied by a disclaimer: 'My Husband hath indeed sometimes said, he would write to you: but hath said again, Mr. *Baxter* will not regard me ... I do not acquaint him with this, but your Advice I know I shall be able to help him

---

[77] Ibid.   [78] Ibid. 190.
[79] Ibid. Lambe's ecclesiological trajectory eventually involved a return to the English state church following his career as a prominent Congregationalist and then Baptist, though he maintained a significant commitment to philanthropy and care for the disadvantaged, as can be seen in his concern for the well-being of prisoners following the Restoration. Kreitzer, 'Thomas Lambe'.
[80] Keeble et al., eds., *Reliquiae Baxterianae*, Vol. 3, 191.   [81] Ibid. 192.   [82] Ibid.
[83] Ibid. 192–3.

by'.[84] She has forwarded a copy of Thomas's arguments, which she asks Baxter to '*peruse, and keep private*'; her second postscript ends: '*I shall long to know that these come safe to your Hands.*'[85]

Barbara's use of the letter is distinctive: she creates a relationship between her husband, an elder in a church of baptised believers, and a prominent writer whom she respects; this is brokered in a way that ensures her agency is not overt. She demonstrates her own expertise in the language of pastoral care, communicating in a register intelligible to her ministerial interlocutor. Barbara is adept at rhetorical persuasion and has deep scriptural knowledge; she also understands the entanglement of theological and personal logistics presented by emotionally freighted doctrines like baptism which had become a conductor for debates about ecclesiology, community formation, and belonging during the Interregnum.

Baxter's reply, on 22 August, confirms the wisdom of Barbara's selection of a pastoral interlocutor and the effective description she provided of her husband's case:

> So much of Christ and his Spirit appeared to me in both your Writings, that my Soul in the reading of them was drawn out into as strong a Stream of Love . . . as almost ever I felt it in my Life. There is a Connaturality of Spirit in the Saints that will work by Sympathy, and by closing uniting Inclinations, through greater Differences and Impediments than the external Act of Baptism.[86]

Baxter notes his familiarity with Thomas's published writing about baptism, having received one of his books from Sir Henry Herbert. He urges that Thomas 'become the Pastor of a Church that's mixt of the Baptized and Re-baptized, if it may be; if not, at least a Publick Preacher in a convenient Station: For I see that Light in his Argumentation, that he may not hide . . . .'[87] Noting that he had received her letter 'near Bed-time on *Saturday* Night, I thought it no Sin to make it part of this Lord's Day's Work to return you this Answer'.[88] Engaging dialogically with Barbara and (through her mediation) with Thomas has made Baxter more conscious of how his published polemic might be interpreted by this particular set of readers. In his postscript he asks that if Thomas '*look into my Book for Infant Baptism, let him know that I much repent of the harsh Language in it, but not of the main matter*'.[89]

Barbara's reply on 4 September clarifies her role in brokering the correspondence between her husband and other key members in this epistolary network. She informs Baxter that she has now told her husband about her letter and shared Baxter's reply with him. Thomas is glad and 'doth entend to writ to you his whole heart', but Barbara manages Baxter's expectations noting that

---

[84] Ibid.   [85] Ibid. 193.   [86] Ibid. 193.   [87] Ibid. 200.   [88] Ibid. 200–1.   [89] Ibid. 201.

Thomas's eighteen-year-old son 'lyes ny unto death'; this has led to a 'present dispouration' which may prevent him from writing immediately.[90] Some who used to hear Thomas will no longer listen 'because of what he hath offered to promote love and good esteem of others'.[91] Indeed, his doubts about baptism are causing them to wonder if there is anything in religion at all. Thomas fears he might be responsible for their apostasy.

The remainder of the letter demonstrates Barbara's theological literacy, her epistolary connections, and her determination to forge links and foster discussion between clergymen as she negotiates shifting beliefs about baptism and their implications for Christian communion. She mentions her friend, Thomas Ledgard, to Baxter: based at Newcastle-upon-Tyne, she has 'had much comunion with [him] in the lord for more then 20 years'.[92] Barbara initiated and maintained theological exchanges with men across England who wrote about the doctrines which preoccupied her and troubled her husband. She is alert to the links between temptation and bodily weakness tracing causal connections in both her husband, Thomas, and her friend, Ledgard's cases. Barbara hopes Baxter's ongoing provision of pastoral care through letters will also attend to such corporeal matters. Later Baxter acknowledged that it was Barbara's suggestion that persuaded him to write to Thomas's ministerial colleague: 'the same woman per*s*waded me to try with Mr *Allen* also: who in conclusion was satisfyed: And they dissolved their Church'.[93]

Several letters from mid-1659 show Baxter continued his epistolary care for Thomas who experienced 'great trouble of Spiritt' despite the change in his views on church communion and baptism, especially as his fears were realised when some members of his credobaptist congregation turned Quaker.[94] Barbara added a short postscript to Thomas's letter of 4 June 1659, that demonstrates her ongoing concern for her husband, and her mediating role within this clergy network. Baxter's '\long letters/ have been of so great use to my Dear husband that I cannot expresse what tharfor I doe owe unto you and unto god for you'.[95] She also asks him to keep providing Thomas with pastoral counsel as he 'is to apt to dispond and doubt wheather god will use him in his service'.[96] Barbara was crucial

---

[90] Keeble & Nuttall, *Calendar*, Vol. 1, 340.   [91] Ibid. 341.

[92] Ledgard's spiritual journey was similar to Thomas Lambe's: he had written against the Quakers; he joined an independent church six years earlier (about the same time the Lambes separated from Goodwin's congregation); he grew 'very ridged in his principiles and spirit', but for the last three years he has had a different vision, 'accompanied with great Temptations and weaknes of body after many letters which I have a mind you \should/ see, he sent us thos enclosed'. Keeble & Nuttall, *Calendar*, Vol. 1, 341. Amongst Baxter's papers is a manuscript entitled 'Church Communion & differences of Judgment Consistent, or A Question resolved' endorsed: 'Mr Ledgards letter to Mrs B. Lambe'. Baxter Treatises, Vol. iv.80.

[93] Keeble et al., eds., *Reliquiae Baxterianae*, Vol. 3, 187.

[94] Keeble & Nuttall, *Calendar*, Vol. 1, 395.   [95] Ibid.   [96] Ibid. 396.

in initiating and sustaining this wider epistolary network focusing on the administration of baptism, defining the church, and nourishing her husband's ministerial vocation and health. Her epistolary interventions shaped how Baxter formulated his pastoral care for her husband's melancholy and his casuistical assessment of Thomas's vocation and responsibilities to the wider communion of saints.

The Communion of Saints within the Republic of Letters: Natural Philosophy, Occasional Meditation, and Pastoral Care

Letter-writing opened a discursive space both metaphorical and material as the circumstances around composition, reception, and reply affected the nature of the real and imagined spaces these epistolary exchanges occurred within and that they generated in turn. The material letter is a form of paperwork. Considering paperwork as a mechanism enabling pastoral care brings the intersectionality of letters as a form of communication, an opportunity for interdisciplinary exchange, and a porous literary genre into focus. Baxter's interest in developments in natural philosophy and the practice of meditation shaped how he provided pastoral care in times of personal grief and political crisis. His correspondence with the natural philosopher, Robert Boyle, demonstrates how epistolary exchange facilitates a methodological interrogation of occasional meditation as a practice drawing on both natural philosophy and theology, and how the act of composing a letter could occasion and incorporate meditation within its literary form. Heterogeneity is characteristic of the letter in seventeenth-century England.[97] While Baxter and Boyle's integration of occasional meditation into the letter as a form of exchange is innovative,[98] Baxter goes further in a letter to Lady Coote, incorporating prayer and eschatological reflection as well, showing how letters of pastoral care actualised the communion of saints, past and present, through combining prayer and paperwork.

Baxter was a self-educated polymath. David Sytsma has demonstrated his detailed critical engagement with new developments in mechanical and Epicurean philosophy and scientific experimentation. Baxter's intellectual trajectory reveals a broad, subtle, and eclectic approach consistently informed by his pastoral concern for the immortal ends of his fellow human beings. Baxter treats humans as embodied creatures functioning within an ecosystem that is both spiritual and material. This underwrites his holistic care for the well-being of those to whom he ministered, carefully calibrated according to 'a divinely ordered hierarchy of goods (God, common good, soul, and body)'.[99] Sytsma notes that Baxter's evaluation of mechanical philosophy was not shared 'by many later

---

[97] See, for example, Hall, 'Epistle'.   [98] Anselment, 'Robert Boyle'.
[99] Sytsma, *Richard Baxter*, 246.

theologians in [his] own tradition', and concludes that such a discontinuity in early modern intellectual history 'warrants greater scholarly attention'.[100] This subsection does not attempt to cover the gap Sytsma identifies. However, Sytsma's detailed recuperative work does emphasise the significance of genre when reflecting on how the process of writing, particularly documents surviving in manuscript rather than print, can reshape scholarly assessments of both historical practices of pastoral care and how they have been reconstituted to support teleological narratives of religious development over time.

Baxter and Boyle had shared interests in biblical translation and missionary activity. In 1661, Baxter provided active support to the Corporation for the Spread of the Gospel in New England, and he recommended Boyle as a worthy governor.[101] He was thanked, in his capacity as Chaplain in Ordinary to Charles II, for his efforts and encouraged to further improve 'the advantage God hath put into [his] hands … by access unto Persons of Honour and Trust' to help secure gospel liberty in New England.[102] This transatlantic endeavour was of long-term interest to Baxter. He wrote to Boyle over two decades later (in 1682) on behalf of the Congregational missionary, John Eliot, requesting permission to print a second edition of his translation of the Bible into Algonquin: 'I intreate you to consider that this question is not whether it be most profitable to the present generation, but whether it shall ever be done.'[103]

These shared interests resulted in an epistolary network that crossed the divide between conformists and nonconformists after the Restoration. As Carol Pal has

---

[100] Ibid. 258.

[101] Keeble & Nuttall, *Calendar*, Vol. 2, 7. This corporation was originally founded in 1649 as the President and Society for the Propagation of the Gospel in New England and was rechartered after the Restoration as the Company for the Propagation of the Gospel in New England and the parts adjacent in America. It remained active in America until 1786. It predates the SPG by over fifty years.

[102] Keeble & Nuttall, *Calendar*, Vol. 2, 19

[103] Keeble & Nuttall, *Calendar*, Vol. 2, 251. See also 248–9. Baxter holds up John Eliot, his Congregational missionary correspondent, as a model in *The Christian Directory*, in order to admonish his readers about the evil of white Protestant European engagement in the capture, traffic, and exploitation of enslaved Africans:

> And on the contrary what an honour is it to those of *New England*, that they take not so much as the Natives Soyl from them, but by purchase? That they enslave none of them, nor use them cruelly, but shew them mercy, and are at a great deal of care and cost and labour for their salvation? O how much difference between holy Master *Eliot*'s life and yours! His, who hath laboured so many years to save them, and hath translated the whole Bible into their language, with other Books; and those good mens in *London* who are a Corporation for the furtherance of his work; and theirs that have contributed so largely towards it; And yours that sell mens souls for your commodity? (p. 558).

This polemical contrast is limited in its historical purview, as Warren has demonstrated in *New England Bound*, 88–91, 96–8.

argued, 'defining intellectual networks according to categories that are both too disparate and too small' can occlude from view the contribution of women and there are similar implications for nonconformists. Letter-writers 'functioned simultaneously in multiple networks', and Pal visualises the republic of letters as 'a palimpsest of translucent and permeable layers'.[104] The horizontal layers are individual networks centred on particular projects (such as scientific experimentation or ecumenism) or identities (for example, radical cults or Huguenot exiles). Scholars strategise and support each other within a horizontal layer but no single layer itself constituted the republic of letters. This means that layers 'must also be visualized as translucent'. Ideas travel vertically connecting members from different horizontal layers to one another and this resulted in the creation of 'new subsets whenever it made sense for the project in question'.[105] Pal's model illuminates Baxter and Boyle's refusal to draw sharp distinctions in their correspondence between observation and experimentalism on scientific or religious grounds. This allows discursive space within their epistolary exchange for pastoral care, and the work of the pastor, to be intimately shaped by developing methods within natural philosophy while respecting the vocational distinction between divine and natural philosopher as discrete spheres of activity.

Baxter's correspondence with Boyle in June/July 1665 was occasioned by an earlier visit where Boyle gave him several of his books.[106] Baxter's letter starts as a note of thanks for: 'Your *Plea for Scripture stile*, and your *Seraphick \Love*, and the noble designe of your Arabicke publication of Grotius, and now your pious *Meditations and Reflexions*.'[107] However, in the process of writing, Baxter's letter develops into a lengthy disquisition on practices of meditation, natural philosophy, and his educational experience, in direct dialogue with Boyle's works, which he has just read, and with Boyle as the imagined epistolary interlocutor. Boyle was astonished to discover that Baxter looked upon the gift of his books 'as a Tempta[t]ion to an over great Esteeme of yourselfe'.[108] Their correspondence about occasional meditation makes clear how integral it was not only to internal disciplining of the self in time management but also to emergent ways of thinking central to both pastoral care and experimental philosophy. This demonstrates how a key element of Baxter's ministry was informed and shaped by developing methodologies of natural philosophy practised by contemporaries like Boyle.[109]

Baxter writes:

---

[104] Pal, *Republic of Women*, 5, 12.   [105] Ibid. 12.
[106] Keeble & Nuttall, *Calendar*, Vol. 2, 43–5.   [107] Ibid. 43.   [108] Baxter Letters ii.287r
[109] Anselment, 'Robert Boyle', 75.

I read your Theologie as the Life of your Philosophie, and your Philosophie as animated and dignifyed by your Theologie; yea indeede as its first part for God himself beginneth the holy scriptures with the doctrine of Physicks: And he that will handle the Covenant and Lawes of God, must describe first the Covenanters *God* and *Man*, the Constitutive parts of the Universal Kingdome: He that will justly frame a *Pansophie* (as Commenius Calls it) must begin with Ontologie; of which God and Man are the parts which we are most Concerned to Know . . .. He that hath well learnt in the Alphabet of his Physicks, wherein a MAN doth differ from a Bruit, hath laid such a foundation for a Holy life, as all the Reason in the world is never able to overthrowe.[110]

This also reveals the porosity between natural philosophy and theology at the heart of Baxter's intellectual development and pastoral practice. Baxter comments not only on the matter of Boyle's *Occasional Meditations* but also on the manner of it. Firstly, because Boyle calls his readers 'to the manly worke of Meditation', and secondly, for his 'special \way/' or method: 'Your examples are the translating of the severall Creatures into a language understood; so that it will teach men when they see the words, (the things) to see withall the *signification* (the *use*): As those that know not only the *Materialls* of an apothecaries shop, but also the *medicinall use* of the simples & compositions'.[111] Boyle's advocacy of meditation is significant, not due to its originality, but because of the weight he gives to 'a way of thinking'.[112]

Baxter is responding to the genre and rhetorical structure of Boyle's *Occasional Meditations* as he writes this letter. These lead him to reflect on his personal experience as an auto-didact, the religious landscape that shaped his thinking – 'when God removed my dwelling into a Churchyard, & sett me to study bones & dust' – and the fragility of human life: 'What a Puppet play is the life of sensuality, worldlynes & pride. & how low a game is it which Emper*ours* & Comm*and*ers play, who seek no higher things, in comparison of a humble Christian, who . . . is seeking the imm*ortall* pleasures?'[113] This fusion of published writings with epistolary exchange demonstrates the shared experimental methodology and associated epistemology embodied in the practice of meditation that lay at the heart of Baxter's concept of the Christian life and which this letter itself exemplifies. Such intersections between the horizontal and vertical layers of the republic of letters reveal the importance of recognising how intellectual and pragmatic friendships operated across Protestant religious divides following the Restoration.

These aspects are further evidenced in Boyle's reply. He expresses appreciation for Baxter's lengthy letter that 'procure[d] mee soe many good Instructi=ons' – implicitly acknowledging the pastoral care intrinsic to Baxter's epistolary

---

[110] Keeble & Nuttall, *Calendar*, Vol. 2, 43–4.   [111] Ibid. 45.
[112] Anselment, 'Robert Boyle', 75.   [113] Keeble and Nuttall, *Calendar*, Vol. 2, 44.

practice.[114] Boyle is grateful for Baxter's receptiveness to his *Occasional Meditations*, for although they have been well received, even by 'divers ... Poets & Wits', several learned men have censured them because they think such compositions unbecoming for the pen of a philosopher.[115] Boyle is indicating his recognition of shared praxis, but also of differing professional priorities, noting that it would be more appropriate for Baxter to write a work of meditations on usual occurrences, as he is already committed to producing further publications on natural philosophy, and the fact that he is not a divine would reduce their public efficacy. However, within the discursive space opened by friendship and epistolary exchange, Boyle acknowledges the enabling fusion of theology and science in the art of meditation rightly practised and communicated:

> It is more my Satisfaction than my Wonder, That you have found an Innocent Divertisement in the perusall of what I have ventur'd to write about Experiment*all* Philosophy, you are too much a Freind to Contempla*t*ion, & too well versd in It, to be an Enemy to that sort of Learning that furnishes it with very Copious & Diffus'd as well as noble Objects. And there are divers things that speake you to be none of those narrow-Sould Divines, that by too much suspecting Naturall Philosophy tempt \many of/ Its Votaries to suspect Theology.[116]

Baxter's provision of holistic pastoral care through letters was inextricably shaped by his passionate, intelligent, and critical engagement with contemporary developments in natural philosophy, particularly in terms of hierarchies of knowledge and the practice of meditation. The latter could cause serious collateral damage – as McKendry has demonstrated[117] – but it also offered intellectual, emotional, and practical solace (Boyle's 'way of thinking') to a diverse range of epistolary correspondents in a period of trauma and change. Baxter never wrote the work of meditations 'upon the most usuall Occurrencyes' that Boyle urged him to undertake. But, in some respects, his letters of pastoral care can be seen to exemplify this exhortation precisely, even if they do so in a different genre. Boyle's *Occasional Meditations* were dedicated to his sister, Lady Ranelagh. Baxter regularly mentions her in his correspondence with Boyle, and there is a scribal copy, in the hand of Margaret, Baxter's wife, of Baxter's letter to Boyle that acknowledges the benefit of Boyle's writings.[118]

---

[114] Baxter Letters ii.287r   [115] Baxter Letters ii.287v.
[116] Keeble & Nuttall, *Calendar*, Vol. 2, 45.   [117] McKendry, *Disavowing Disability*, 5.
[118] Keeble & Nuttall, *Calendar*, Vol. 2, 43, 45. Katherine Ranelagh was closely connected to her brother, Robert Boyle, running a scientific salon, as well as being a neighbour of John Milton. Ibid. 67. Women such as Ranelagh, Gell, and Margaret Baxter were integral to the formation of networks that facilitated scientific and theological enquiry and the provision of pastoral care.

The dialogical nature of epistolary exchange can elide the distinction between occasional meditation and letter in a way that reveals the rich synergy emerging from theology's engagement with natural philosophy that both Baxter and Boyle attest to. This generic porosity can be seen in a letter that Baxter sent to Lady Coote several years later. Baxter did not know of her until Lady Parsons provided directions for him to receive a legacy from Coote's recently deceased husband, Colonel Chidley Coote. Baxter's letter begins with an acknowledgement of gratitude: 'The obliga=tion hereby laid upon me a Stranger & undeserving did bind me to Endeavour to know what credible fame would make knowne of you both.'[119] His enquiries led him to learn of Lady Coote's recent loss and his expression of thankfulness for material networks of caregiving (communicated via letter) morphs into an epistolary meditation on eternity and the nature of the soul. As Baxter writes this letter, he envisages such meditations as a profitable pastoral and textual intervention due to Coote's personal grief and (as members of the fragile communion of saints networked across the British archipelago) a suitable response to their shared political and religious disappointments.

> And what is a world so deserted but the suburbs or outer part of Hell. When our little remain\[in]g/ light is extinguished, where are we but in outer darkness? . . .. But like will to like: all the Elements have an aggregative motion: & all the parts would be together: ffire wil be no lon=ger kept with us here below, than the charme of its disposed. fewell doth detaine it (or imprison it) So Holy Soules would be with God. The father of Spirits sent us not into the lower wor[l]d to dwell or stay or rest: But a while to animate a Materiall Body, & in it to pass through Certaine tryalls, & do such workes as he is pleased in; to fill us for our true & endless rest . . .. Madam! W[ha]t hearts should you & I have if we saw the things which we (too weakely) believe? If we saw whither all departed soules go, & where our old companions are & w[ha]t they now Enjoy & do? . . .. should we (think you) more desire them to be ag[ai]n with us, or rather that we might speedyly be with them?[120]

Baxter complements this shared grief and imagined future with a reference to Dr Henry Hammond's translation of resurrection from the Greek noting that it 'doth not onely signify the *last* resurrection . . . but that it often signifieth . . . the *next life*, or *state of* the *soul immediately after death*; or *our succeeding state of life*: This is the happyness of a soul that here liveth a heavenly life'.[121] Baxter combines direct address to Lady Coote with a shared positionality: 'we saw', 'our old companions', but he is also willing to draw on contemporary interpretations of New Testament Greek with an unknown female correspondent. The conclusion of the letter is a prayer, demonstrating how Baxter seamlessly

---

[119] Baxter Letters iv.39r.   [120] Ibid.   [121] Keeble & Nuttall, *Calendar*, Vol. 2, 71–2.

integrated eschatology, contemporary politics, counsel for grief, natural philosophy, biblical scholarship, and an empathetic engagement with the particularities of his imagined interlocutor into a distinctive blend of literary caregiving: 'This is the best on earth which I can desire for my self, & therfore for any other: t[ha]t we may be followers of them who through faith & patience inherit the p[ro]mises & have past the dangers which we have yet to pass.'[122] Baxter's letter also draws the epistolary network of earthly correspondents into communion with those in heaven.

Epistolary Casuistry, Restoration Censorship, and Caring for (Pastoral) Caregivers

Baxter was a recognised authority on pastoral care, due to his own successful ministry in Kidderminster, and his many published books, especially *Gildas Salvianus*, when he was no longer employed by the state church due to stipulations the restored regime made for conformity in the early 1660s. However, he continued to fulfil the role of pastor to pastors of varying partisan identities after the Restoration and this reveals much about how he, and his correspondents, conceptualised and practised pastoral care and the ways in which it could, and sometimes could not, be communicated through letters. The privations Baxter faced placed material and imaginative restrictions on the type of discursive spaces he could generate or engage with through epistolary exchange. The choice of a correspondent to remain anonymous, or communicate via a proxy, also challenged the creation of a shared discursive space for the provision of pastoral care through letters, and Baxter is clear about how both censorship and the assumption of anonymity shaped his epistolary practice.

Baxter identifies in his memoir, *Reliquiae Baxterianae*, how his nonconformity exposed him to surveillance and resulted in significant self-censorship that meant he was unable to participate in the European republic of letters in the way that other scholars and ministers expected of him:

> divers Forreign Divines had written to me, and expected such Correspondence as Literate Persons have with one another: But I knew so well what eyes were upon me, and how others had been used in some such accounts, that I durst not write one Letter to any beyond the Seas: By which some were offended, as little knowing our Condition here.[123]

One such correspondent was the Swiss pastor, Johann Zollikofer (1633–92), who wrote to Baxter in April 1663, asking his 'Advice about setting up the Work of Ministerial Instruction of the Families and Persons of their Charge … but

---

[122] Baxter Letters iv.39v.　　[123] Cited by Keeble & Nuttall, *Calendar*, Vol. 2, 34.

I sent him an Answer by his Friend by word of mouth only.'[124] It can be inferred that this friend was Mr Dorvile, to whose 'care' Zollikofer recommends his letter.[125] Care is invoked here at several levels: Zollikofer is seeking advice on how a minister who does not have the support of his colleagues in the work of personal instruction should proceed in relation to this aspect of pastoral care that was critical to Baxter's own professional practice; Zollikofer relies on the care of his friend in ensuring that his letter is delivered safely to Baxter; Baxter relies on the care of a friend to pass on by word of mouth the response that he is careful not to put in writing; Baxter takes care to reproduce Zollikofer's letter in full as part of his posthumous memoir in an attempt to ensure that an accurate narrative of nonconformist experience and experiments in pastoral care is preserved for posterity.

The letter also reveals Baxter's centrality within a network of godly ministers and correspondents that stretched across the Swiss Confederacy, Europe, and North America. Zollikofer visited England for ten months to learn English in 1656 and his *Album amicorum* lists John Milton, John Dury, Lady Ranelagh, John Owen, and John Wilkins amongst the friends he made then, but not Baxter.[126] However, two of his cousins are visiting London and this allows Zollikofer to communicate to Baxter the high regard he has for him, which is shared by 'our Neighbour Protestant Confederate Cities of *Zuric* and *Schaffhousen*'.[127] The respect in which Baxter is held by Swiss Protestants was based on a detailed knowledge of his published works, especially *Saints' Rest* and *Gildas Salvianus*. Zollikofer 'cannot express the great Advantage I received by them: so that I commended the very same Books to others of our Brethren who have endeavoured without delay to get them, by means of some of our Merchants here; and also the remainder of your Works, that we could bring to our notice ... For which Works we thank God with one accord'. He notes that in *Gildas Salvianus* 'you strike home to the very heart many Ministers'.[128] This international testimony to the influence of his publications on the pastoral care he had modelled in his own ministry in Kidderminster was clearly important to Baxter, as he preserved and reproduced this letter as part of his memoir, but the constraints on his participation as a pastor and scholar within the republic of letters are also demonstrated by his refusal to commit to a reply in writing in 1663. Zollikofer also asks 'whether it is really true that through the restoration of episcopacy Presbyterian ministers are prevented from exercising their ministries' and if 'Popery may be introduced into England.'[129] Baxter's failure to respond speaks volumes, but so does his decision to publish this as part of his personal history of the British Civil Wars. Baxter's best-selling

---

[124] Ibid. 38.   [125] Ibid.   [126] Ibid.   [127] Ibid.   [128] Ibid. 38–9.   [129] Ibid. 39

publications, set alongside his extensive correspondence network, demonstrate the critical role that epistolarity played in forming and enhancing his international reputation for pastoral care, and his increasing significance as an exemplar for pastors on practices of catechising and caregiving.

Despite his nonconformity, and the censorship and persecution this entailed, Baxter remained an important connection between elite networks of power, sources of patronage, and a wider diaspora of nonconformist Protestant ministers across the British Atlantic. John Eliot's approach to Baxter requesting support for a second edition of his translation of scripture in Algonquin is one instance of this considered already. But Baxter's influence as an exemplar of, and patron for, pastoral care operated at multiple levels within the republic of letters. On 3 April 1669, Matthew Hill, a curate of Thirsk, Yorkshire, from 1657 until his ejection, wrote to Baxter from Maryland, noting he was indebted to Baxter for 'the meanes off my new liffe and lively hood', but that he has 'not yet done begging', as he is not able to purchase 'such bookes as are usefull and necessary ffor my worke'.[130] Hill sends his letter by a young gentleman, who is able to provide a full account of his country and affairs. Hill asks that any response to his request be sent via this messenger. Hill also notes that Baxter's letter to and interest with a Mr Davy and his wife was so successful in advocating for him that they supported his journey from England to North America. This experience encourages Hill to request further assistance, particularly through the provision of books, but also that Baxter advocate on Hill's behalf with any brethren or friends who might have the ability and heart to help those who stand in need. The presence of a chosen bearer for this letter carries expectation of a return; Hill notes that he cannot purchase anything in Virginia until the tobacco is harvested – it being the only current money in that province.[131] The material conditions of composition, reception, and transmission are integral to the shared discursive space within which their epistolary exchange operates.

Hill describes at some length the situation he finds himself in as a nonconformist English expatriate in Maryland, then under the governance of Lord Baltimore. As a Catholic governor, Baltimore provides public freedom of religion. Hill rejoices in this and hopes that it will make his work more successful, as the people are not fond of liturgy or ceremonies. He notes that two or three itinerant preachers from amongst the young men in England who want wages and cannot work would be instrumental in helping the people in Maryland, whom he judges to be of free disposition and kind to their ministers. He again pleads with Baxter to act on his behalf to achieve this outcome.

---

[130] Ibid. 72–3.   [131] Baxter Letters iii.261–2.

As with several of the SPG's early missionaries, it is the Celtic fringes of Britain that proved to be one of the best sources of young men willing to engage in ministry overseas. Hill observes: 'wee have many also off the rifformed religion, who have a long while lived as sheepe without a shepherd tho last yeare brought in a young man ffrom Ireland, who hath already had good successe in his worke'.[132] Hill's letter demonstrates the extensive reach of Baxter's epistolary caregiving and the expectations of practical support that it generated. Hill's move to Maryland takes him into settler zones with new opportunities for ministry, but very limited financial resources. However, despite this change in Hill's pastoral identity and geographical location, there is a real sense of continuity, both in terms of his sense of vocation and responsibility for the communities around him, and in the assumption of reciprocity and provision between the old world and the new. Baxter is expected to activate his patronage networks via letter on Hill's behalf to provide books and funds, and more broadly, England (or the British archipelago), is seen to bear a responsibility to provide trained itinerant ministers to meet the spiritual needs of British immigrants of a reformed persuasion in Virginia.

Different, but equally challenging, were some of the practical issues that nonconformity in England during the Restoration presented to conscientious pastors advising scrupulous congregants – many of these ministers wrote to Baxter asking for guidance, an implicit invitation for pastoral care through letters. Baxter's letter to an unidentified person responding to a manuscript, not extant, probably sent c. 1669 or later demonstrates the difficulties that nonconformists faced in both establishing identified places of worship and in working out what responsibilities belonged to specific people to provide ministry and pastoral care during periods of persecution with penal legislation in place against corporate gatherings. Baxter distinguishes between those responsibilities that are proper to the ministerial function and those which are shared with others: the latter may be performed by masters in their families, or any Christian occasionally, but the former cannot. He also notes that it is important to distinguish between ordinary cases and extraordinary in necessity, 'as if a private [Christ]ian learned & able were cast amongst the In=dians, who doubteth but he may teach daily & publiquely'. This demonstrates how exposure to England's North American colonies challenged Baxter to reimagine what pastoral care might involve in very different logistical and social circumstances. He also recognises that a 'like necessity' could fall out 'nearer home'. On the question of places for worship, Baxter notes that the temple was divinely appointed by God for Jewish worship, but this is not the case now, suggesting that it is for the Christian magistracy to determine these. It is clear from the letter that Baxter does not know

---

[132] Baxter Letters iii.261r.

who has authored the manuscript and he is willing to deal with this person by way of controversy and a full answer (forms of caregiving in their own right) only if his correspondent 'subscribe[s] his name'.[133] Anonymity prevents the reader/recipient/ respondent from evaluating 'how care sits in a geography of relationship' and thus constrains the creation of a shared discursive space through epistolary exchange.[134]

Anonymity is again invoked in a letter that Baxter wrote to a minister on 29 April 1669. Baxter's reply acknowledges that the original letter (not extant) was received about a month after it was written on 25 March, as he was 'neere 30 miles from home', probably staying with Richard Hampden.[135] Baxter begins somewhat testily: 'About [th]e case you mention I suppose thay knowe my ju\d/gment but I had rather have had the direction from themselves that to them I might have returned my answer, but having them from you, I answer them to you'.[136] This differs dramatically from how Baxter responded to Barbara Lambe's brokerage of epistolary exchange, and anonymity is the sticking point – Baxter cannot imagine his multiple interlocutors. The proffered case relates to how one may lawfully engage in participating in communion and Baxter suggests: 'if any of them scruple kneeling though not in eating but in taking, I suppose you may connive at them without danger, for in the publicke assemblies of london few kneele that I can perseive; and I never heard of any questioned for giving it them'.[137] The receiving of the sacrament is essential to most Protestant models of Christian life and practice: administration of baptism and communion was particularly difficult for English nonconformists; Baxter here indicates his acute recognition of the challenges nonconformity presented for both those receiving and giving communion. It was also something that Baxter and his household had to negotiate and he draws on his own practice as a model for dealing with such complex questions of conscience as 'the best parte of my advice to others'.[138] Remote casuistry based on personal experience is here transmuted through the technology of the letter as an act of pastoral care to an anonymous enquirer via a ministerial advocate, who also uses a letter to present the case on behalf of their contact. Baxter describes his own practice thus: 'if I have opertunity to have stated communion with a church well disciplined, I will bee ordinarily there: But yet once or twice a yeare I would communicate with an undisciplined church, yea with an independent or an honest Anabaptist church, to shew my judgment by my practise, that I hould not communion with them to bee simply unlawfull, nor seperate from any christians further then they seperate from christ, nor

---

[133] Keeble & Nuttall, *Calendar*, Vol. 2, 67; Baxter Letters ii.110r.
[134] Bunting, *Labours of Love*, 6.   [135] Keeble & Nuttall, *Calendar*, Vol. 2, 73.
[136] Baxter Letters v.210r.   [137] Keeble & Nuttall, *Calendar*, Vol. 2, 73.
[138] Baxter Letters v.210r.   .

reject them further then christ rejecteth them. And rather than com*m*unicate noe where at all, I would constantly com*m*unicate with such ....'[139]

Baxter notes, however, that it is very difficult to keep those who have been injured from passions that hinder the exercise of their understanding. He cannot expect that the short epistolary account of his judgement, despite all his interest in the case his correspondent has raised, will satisfy the relevant parties, unless he were present in person. This leads Baxter to reveal his exasperation at the failure of the restored episcopal establishment to attend to his advice:

> I tould [th]e B[isho]ps at first that when the ministers were expelled, the people (partly as unguided and partly as Exasp[er]ated would run much further from them then thay are: But thay thought t[he]ms[elves] wiser than to beleve mee, and were confident that if thay could have gott away their former Teachers as farr from them as since thay have done, the people would have bine all conformable. And others neere you of t[ha]t opinion have tryed the same way. But woe to that people on whom either pastors or physicians must try experim==ents to procure wisdom, and that must pay so deare for [th]e learning of their guides! and yet thay are loathe to leave their error to this day but thinke that the sword would heale our wounds. But I hope god hath taught you that what is not to be done by Reason and Love is not to bee done at all by pastors; and accordingly to exercise convincing and paternall conduct.[140]

Baxter indicts the bishops for their failure to provide pastoral care through the re-established state church. He also sets out his own understanding of what constitutes effective pastoral care. Baxter wants his clerical colleagues to use reason and love to establish the right relationships for pastoral caregiving. Pastoral power remains implicit as Baxter notes the importance of 'convincing and paternall conduct' on the part of the minister. But he is scathing in his assessment of the collateral damage done by 'pastors or physicians' who 'must try experim==ents to procure wisdom'; this remains a consistent component of his critique of the state church's failure to provide pastoral care after the Restoration.

Baxter's postscript is telling as it invokes the sense of a tradition of epistolary caregiving within Reformed Protestantism demonstrating the enduring value of letters that deal pastorally with challenges which recur in the lives of Christians when facing persecution or exile, regardless of the location in space and time of the believer negotiating these: 'some of calvines epistles when he was expelled geneva and some others questioned com*m*unicating with the ministers and people that expelled him, do represent your neighbours case and mine so

---

[139] Keeble & Nuttall, *Calendar*, Vol. 2, 73.   [140] Baxter Letters v.210r–210v.

exactly, that I could wish I had time to translate one or two of them for their use'.[141] It also demonstrates the limits that Baxter occasionally imposed on himself when attempting to assess anonymous cases of conscience transmitted by letter that carried an implicit expectation that he would respond to any epistolary invitation to provide pastoral care. This refusal to engage in epistolary translation is an unusual example of Baxter momentarily practising selfcare in his role as a pastoral counsellor.

2 The Incorporated Company and Epistolary Care

This section considers the experimental, imaginative, and exploitational provision of pastoral care through letters written by the SPG in partnership with missionaries, schoolteachers, volunteers, subscribers, and church officials from various Protestant groups following its foundation in 1701. The discourses of pastoral care created and curated through and beyond these epistolary exchanges include frequent references to broader non-literate congregations or populations defined as potential objects of care. The SPG's status as an incorporated company allowed an apparently seamless fusion of 'charitable impulses with commercial ambitions in their activities'.[142] Its incorporated structure enabled it to absorb legal bequests which meant that its provision of pastoral care through letters was partly resourced by violent expropriation of enslaved labour; it also facilitated the development of bureaucratic structures that crisscrossed the British Atlantic administering global missions through a dense network of correspondents. Over its first two decades the SPG created a transatlantic network of care built on the intersection between benevolence and enslavement.

In order to examine how the SPG functions as a *persona ficta* enabling a material and metaphorical discursive space to be imagined and established by engaging its missionary employees and interlocutors in epistolary exchange, I consider a small portion of manuscript correspondence written by the SPG's earliest colonial missionaries. Letters, as a textual technology capable of travelling across liminal geographical zones, resourced the pastoral caregiving of these missionaries and enabled specific forms of agency and engagement. The letters missionaries sent and received textually shaped and mediated relationships between religious practice, enslavement, ethnographic reflection, professional advancement, conversion, and corporate control, to forge new forms of pastoral caregiving through paperwork chains of correspondence across the British Atlantic.

---

[141] Keeble & Nuttall, *Calendar*, Vol. 2, 73–4.   [142] Yamamoto, *Taming Capitalism*, 249.

Corporations

John Kettlewell's gloss on Philippians 3:20 in *Of Christian Communion* (1693) set out a biblical rationale for a heavenly corporation that had immediate implications for its earthly participants. Thomas Bray, the SPG's founder, recommended Kettlewell's scriptural exegesis, which defined corporation as follows:

> And of the Unity of this Church, or Collection of all Believers, do those Scriptures speak, which represent all that are in Heaven and all that are in Earth, as one whole Family. Eph. 3. 15. As one House-hold. 1 Tim. 3. 15. and Gal. 6. 10. or, as one City, Heb. 12. 22. Whence accordingly all, who are at any time in this world, are said to have their Citizenship or Corporation in Heaven, Phil. 3. 20. And all who are admitted into Christs Church here, to be Fellow-Citizens with the Saints, and Domesticks with Prophets, and Apostles, and with all others, who are gone to God before. Eph. 2. 19. What is the one Body, saith St Chrysostom on the words of St. Paul, there is one Body? 'Tis all believers, of every place, saith he, both those who now are, and who formerly have been, and who hereafter shall be.[143]

This passage conflates an entire 'set of social groupings: citizenship, aligned with corporation (presumably the urban corporation), is mentioned twice, alongside family and household ('domestick'). In doing so, Kettlewell suggests an equivalence between these ways of forming, and belonging to, social groups, in order to emphasise the idea of unity'.[144] The theme of incorporation, as David D. Hall observes, 'acquired a fresh significance' after many disruptions, such as 'old world to new, parish church to gathered', 'for on it depended the future health (spiritual and otherwise) of family, child, church and colony'.[145]

Corporations drove economic growth and English territorial expansion in Ireland, the Americas, Africa, and East Asia. They fostered the development of experimental and exploitative forms of cultural expression, by allowing religion, trade, and national identity to be reconceptualised in new forms.[146] The colonies were laboratories for religious experimentation,[147] acting as critical counterpoints to the revolutionary and nonconformist innovations explored via epistolary caregiving in seventeenth-century England. Corporations, such as the SPG, provide an integral link between the use of letters as a surrogate form of pastoral caregiving and surveillance via paper networks and technologies stimulated by revolution and Restoration, examined in Section 1, and the new bureaucratic networks of pastoral care created across the British Atlantic considered here. Such epistolary caregiving often involved redefining boundary

---

[143] Cited by Haydon, *Corporate Culture*, 165–6.   [144] Ibid. 166.
[145] Hall, 'Puritanism in a Local Context', 81.   [146] Haydon, *Corporate Culture*, 182.
[147] Games, *The Web of Empire*, 251.

markers such as baptism, church membership, and ordination, which remained pressure points in England, the Caribbean, and North America. These markers of identity and transition were integral to the practice of pastoral care and helped to define who was (or was not) an appropriate recipient of specific forms of pastoral care. Recent work demonstrates the central and flexible role corporations, such as the SPG (and its chaplains and missionaries), played in mediating relationships between church and state, the individual and the collective, the nation-state and the commercial activities of its members in other jurisdictions between 1650 and 1720.[148]

Analysing how the SPG's missionaries used letters to create effective and affective forms of caregiving contributes to our understanding of 'the role of religion in corporate sociology'.[149] Such letters were essential to the personal and pastoral identity, authority, and well-being of early missionaries. The corporation, as a *persona ficta*, mediated between reality and fiction transforming 'ideas of fellowship, commonwealth, nation or belief into reality as an enduring institutional form'.[150] The SPG archive demonstrates how essential letters as a technology were in enabling the solicitation, administration, and provision of pastoral care, and in creating and establishing the SPG as a significant entity in the early modern British Atlantic. Letters were central to how the SPG conceptualised itself from the start, not least because it consisted of people continually moving. Given the absence of colonial bishops, the geographically disparate programme of the SPG 'depended on correspondence to make plans drawn up in London a reality'. Employees were instructed and superintended by letters; supporters were solicited by letters; the letters missionaries sent back 'were at the heart of this system'. The SPG's 'reporting requirements made reflecting on and writing about the condition of local non-European people part of missionaries' routine responsibilities; they also framed and limited those reflections in certain ways'.[151]

Missionaries and clergy wrote to the SPG in expansive and confessional terms. They sought 'financial aid and practical advice, defended their reputations, lamented their troubles, and offered suggestions based on their experiences. Many simply looked to retain connections to the lives they had left behind . . . . These webs of correspondence carried missionary strategies, attitudes toward slavery, views on the origins of Native Americans, and a host of other ideas around the Atlantic world'.[152] Epistolary connections were

---

[148] Pettigrew & Veevers, eds., *The Corporation as a Protagonist*; Yamamoto, *Taming Capitalism*. For a consideration of mission agencies as adjuncts to church structures operating in liminal spaces, see Smith, 'Positioning Missionaries' and Arthur, 'The Future of Mission Agencies'.
[149] Smith, 'Religion', 137.   [150] Haydon, *Corporate Culture*, 10.
[151] Glasson, *Mastering Christianity*, 35.   [152] Ibid.

coordinated and controlled by the SPG Secretary and, consequently, 'decisions about whom to convert and how to go about doing it were never made in isolation or just in the colonies but were rather the product of transatlantic discussion and debate'.[153] The technology of the letter facilitated such paper exchanges over distance, and the process of writing invited imaginative participation on the part of writer and recipient, each conscious of their contribution to a charitable corporation responsible for creating and administering a new transatlantic community of care, which produced a discursive space both metaphorical and material centred on and coordinated by the Secretary as the SPG's representative. The Secretary 'was responsible for maintaining the transatlantic and domestic correspondences essential to [the SPG's] activities'. Secretaries often served for a long time, were 'best placed to understand' the breadth of the SPG's business, and 'wielded a considerable amount of authority as sources of institutional memory' and as the main go-between the missionaries and membership.[154]

Liam Haydon warns that focusing on the 'voluminous archives' that corporations have left behind, including the many 'fascinating and worthwhile stories' they contain carries certain risks. Such archives do not 'help us understand the circulation of their ideas' resulting in corporate histories that offer a 'functional vision', overlooking 'the cultural biases of their protagonists in favour of . . . explanations of action centred on economics or other self-interest'.[155] The charitable focus of the SPG means it has not been subjected to functional economic interpretations in the same way as early modern corporations with a clear commercial agenda. Haydon notes that the use of incorporated companies as a vehicle for charitable as well as commercial operations is increasingly rare now, resulting in an impoverishment of corporate imagery and how it functions within the broader culture. Tracing how the SPG's epistolary network contributed to emerging ideologies and practices of pastoral care in the British Atlantic helps to enrich and expand our understanding of corporate history.[156] Letters were both objects in themselves and a gloss on, or index to, other objects.[157] The material letters exchanged by the SPG and their missionaries curated administrative expectations, figures and accounts; details about varying cultural practices, including the indigenous and enslaved populations that the

---

[153] Ibid. 36   [154] Ibid. 25. For a similar model see Russell, *Being a Jesuit*, 6.
[155] Haydon, *Corporate Culture*, 185.   [156] Ibid. 186–7.
[157] Ferlier examines 'the practicalities of the distribution and collection of books in the establishment of Protestant networks across the Atlantic' (p. 33), with a particular focus on Quakers and Anglicans, including the libraries of SPG founder, Thomas Bray. 'For . . . transatlantic missions to be successful, the proselytes first had to establish reliable networks of exchange, so that men, goods and news reached both sides of the ocean' (p. 34). 'Building Religious Communities with Books'.

SPG sought to subject to the care of the English state church; medical and sacramental provision; and religious controversies, particularly with nonconformist Protestant groups who were often well-established in North American and Caribbean colonies. These letters also acted as indices to care packages of books, catechisms, and other artefacts considered essential to ritual practice, jointly providing a material underwriting of Anglican clerical identity and power and authorising the SPG's provision of parochial oversight to a contested range of care recipients. Letters, as a form of paperwork, and a technology for communication, were essential to the formation and sustenance of this emerging network of care.

Enslavement

The flexibility of corporate structures to facilitate transactions within and beyond the nation-state also led to complex entanglements. Simon Gikandi argues that narratives of aesthetics and enslavement need to be connected to understand how Christopher Codrington was constructed as an English gentleman and a man of taste, as even those who join the two 'find it more convenient to describe Codrington's philanthropy as "aberrancy" rather than to locate it in the logic of the slave master trying to refashion his identity within the culture of taste'.[158] Philanthropy is not only linked to the culture of taste, it also triangulates the relationships with slavery and aesthetics, commerce and culture. These can be traced in how Codrington framed his will which, in 1710, bequeathed two slavery plantations in Barbados to the fledgling SPG, setup less than a decade earlier to promote mission rather than commerce. This bequest irrevocably shaped the SPG's financial resourcing, future development, and how it provided pastoral care across the British Atlantic: 'Christopher Codrington – perhaps based on his experience of living among enslaved West Africans – wanted his college to produce missionaries with medical training so they could "Both indear themselves to the People and have the better oppertunitys of doeing good To mens Souls whilst they are Takeing Care of their Bodys"'.[159] The moral complexity of this freighted legacy and its implications for understanding pastoral care requires a consideration of missionary philanthropy, as well as Enlightenment aesthetics, and its repressed other, enslavement.

Aesthetics are a critical concern, not least because the SPG's correspondence is analysed here as a form of literary caregiving. But, as the Introduction set out, the discursive formulation of racialised colonial subjects within distorted theologies, the entanglements of settler zones with shifting agencies, loyalties and power bases, emergent discourses of humanitarianism within the broader

---

[158] Gikandi, *Slavery and the Culture of Taste*, 122.   [159] Glasson, *Mastering Christianity*, 164.

publics of Britain's nascent imperial reach, and the racial, patriarchal, imperial, and class hierarchies that shaped the creation, preservation, and curation of archival documents, and who could access them, impact in intimate, profound, and intangible ways the accounts of the past that have been given, and which can be written:[160] 'The irony is dark and yet unambiguous: the most self-sacrificing, faithful, and zealous missionaries in the Atlantic world formulated and theorized a powerful and lasting religious ideology for a brutal system of plantation labor'.[161]

Annette Laing postulates that while missionaries saw Anglicanism as a complete package, 'it would be more helpful to view it as did many white lay folk as well as Africans in early South Carolina. They understood the Church of England's offerings to be a collection of spiritual services from which they could select at will as they created religious observances that were meaningful to them'. Laing suggests that those 'Africans who were exposed (indirectly or directly) to Anglican Christianity' regarded it as they did 'all potential spiritual tools: selectively and constructively, not necessarily as a conscious form of resistance to slavery and white society but as a means to control their everyday environments'.[162] Institutional slavery shaped the lives of enslaved people in different ways to those owned by an individual master or mistress; this could have a significant impact on the material and emotional aspects of their daily life.[163] The SPG's role as an institutional owner, claiming (falsely) to act as a benevolent example of plantation management, is significant in this broader polemical context of race, status, religious mission, and philanthropy. Indeed, distinctions between freedom and bondage in the early modern British Atlantic were complex: nationality, religion, poverty, war, and other factors could determine one's status as enslaved or free alongside race. This will be examined in relation to Elias Neau, the Huguenot prisoner, French merchant, naturalised English subject, and SPG catechist to enslaved people considered later. Gikandi identifies the sharp edge of this sliding scale for interpersonal and race relations in the early modern Caribbean and North America:

> Quite often, debates on the nature of African slavery in the new world were prefaced by the necessity to affirm the distinctiveness of an English identity that had to account for its presence and prescience in zones of displacement and enslavement .... The greatest anxieties about freedom were often expressed by those invested in the enslavement of others as if they, the free, might fall into the condition that sustained their lives ... The existence of

---

[160] For a polemical interrogation, see Mohamed, 'On Race and Historicism'.
[161] Gerbner, *Christian Slavery*, 196.   [162] Laing, '"Heathens and Infidels"?', 200–1.
[163] Oast, *Institutional Slavery*.

slavery clarified the meaning of freedom. As the English exiles in Barbados realized, freedom could best be imagined and desired when slavery was witnessed as its radical other.[164]

Yet, as Neau and others discovered, forms of slavery were not necessarily radically other for some exiles and European expatriates in the early modern British Atlantic.[165]

The SPG and Its Early Missionaries in North America

The network of pastoral caregiving through letters which the SPG created in its first two decades from c. 1701–20 is assessed by tracing the careers, lived experiences, and correspondence of several early missionaries from different backgrounds operating across North America: George Keith, the Scottish Quaker and belated convert to Anglicanism, and his compatriot geographer and missionary, Patrick Gordon; the French Huguenot, merchant and catechist to enslaved Africans in New York, Elias Neau; and Dr Francis Le Jau, another former French Huguenot, ministering in the parish of St James, part of the fledgling Anglican establishment in South Carolina. Collectively these epistolary exchanges demonstrate the material and emotional stakes of pastoral caregiving across a broad geography on the eastern seaboard of North America, encompassing both urban and rural parishes, as well as different pastoral roles: missionary-priest, itinerant missionary, and catechist. New forms of bureaucratic accountability for the selection, training, funding, and pastoral practice of missionaries were primarily created and interrogated through pastoral letters as a genre. The process of writing and exchanging such letters disciplined and shaped ideas of self, other, and community.

At the centre of these webs of correspondence stretching across the Atlantic was the SPG's Secretary, John Chamberlayne, who served as the inaugural incumbent from 1702–11. He helped create the administrative structures that shaped the SPG's provision of pastoral care in operational terms.[166] These are evidenced in the extensive archive of incoming correspondence, which often bears annotations indicating the sender's identity and date received, and copies of outgoing correspondence. Chamberlayne's copy of his letter responding to a verbal complaint passed on by Mr Jones that the Archbishop of Cashel had not

---

[164] Gikandi, *Slavery and the Culture of Taste*, 32–3.

[165] Smith, 'Between the Galley and Plantation', 26; Urvashi Chakravarty explores the slippage between service, servitude, and slavery in the early modern British Atlantic in *Fictions of Consent*.

[166] Cf. with a successor, David Humphreys, the SPG Secretary from 1716–40, 'who does not seem to have been disposed to answer letters while holding this post, but he probably managed the society's affairs efficiently since by the year after his death its income had risen by 50 per cent'. Archbold & Cowie, 'Humphreys, David (1690–1740)', *ODNB*.

heard from him for a long time provides a concrete insight into his correspondence practices as the SPG's Secretary after he had occupied the role for some seven years:

> I don't find that I ever had the Honour of more than three L[ett]ers from your Grace, which as they are enter'd upon my Books bear date 25th ffeb[rua]ry 1706/ 24 June 1707. & 26 Aug[us]t. all which I answered very punctually, and hope that all my answers, especially the last came safe to Your Grace's hands . . .. Thus I think stands the State of our Correspondence my Lord, for after all I dare not peremptorily affirm that it is so, for unless I kept Copies of all the Letters I writ (which in my great and diffused Correspondence in so many parts of the World wou'd be endless) I cou'd not be positive of such a matter; and this is the reason too that I cannot write so often as I wou'd, did I follow my own Inclina= =nation, especially to such Illustrious Corres= =pondents as your Grace.[167]

Alongside the patronage of Archbishop Thomas Tenison,[168] the Bishop of London, Henry Compton, and the work of the first Treasurer, John Hodges, Chamberlayne's linguistic and organisational skills were integral to establishing and implementing the SPG as it was originally conceptualised by Thomas Bray.

The activities of this elite group of men in London need to be positioned within several wider cultural developments. Regardless of their individual political allegiances and the shifting vicissitudes of court favour, the SPG's practices were shaped by innovations in ruling via paper,[169] the overlapping philosophical, religious, and medical interests of the republic of letters, and the intersections between an imperative to convert enslaved people and the development of laws across the British Atlantic that helped to define and entrench racial slavery as a social institution.[170] The limitations of the early SPG archive, with surviving documents written largely from white, Eurocentric, Christian perspectives, are acknowledged, as is the intensive use of these documents for telling various kinds of histories about the early British Atlantic, particularly the North American colonies. The focus here is on how letters – the central genre surviving from the first two decades of the SPG's existence – were written, exchanged, read, and curated as a mechanism for providing pastoral care, and enacting pastoral power.

---

[167] SPG 8 90. John Chamberlayne to the Archbishop of Cashel. Dated 14 May 1709. In a postscript Chamberlayne notes that he is preparing 'another little packet for your Grace'.

[168] 'Certainly his work for the [SPG] was substantial; a contemporary spoke of his practical wisdom as president, putting "a stop to many indirect motions and steps made to put us out of the way"'. Marshall, 'Tenison, Thomas (1636–1715)', *ODNB*.

[169] See, for example, Siddique, 'The Archival Epistemology'; 'Governance Through Documents'.

[170] Foote, *Black and White Manhattan*, 196.

George Keith and Patrick Gordon: Establishing the Communication Framework Between Metropolitan Centre and Colonial Peripheries

There was a significant porosity of allegiance within and beyond the state church in England's North American colonies, and the SPG drew ecumenically on various Protestant groups when selecting its early missionaries. This can be seen in the decision to employ George Keith, a former Quaker, and surveyor, with a detailed knowledge of North America, and his fellow Scot, Patrick Gordon, a geographer, whose tenure as a missionary was very brief. Keith had extensive knowledge of the colonies from his period there as a surveyor, schoolteacher, and prominent Friend. His conversion to the Church of England in the mid-1690s meant that he was a well-informed, indefatigable, and committed missionary and controversialist for the SPG from 1702 to 1704, uniquely equipped and experienced in utilising print resources, communication networks, and letters, to achieve the goals of the newly formed SPG.[171] Keith was formative in shaping the contours of the SPG's mission through a campaign of itinerant preaching in areas where Anglicans faced significant competition from other Protestant denominations for the hearts and purses of European settlers.

Patrick Gordon published his initial 'Proposals for Propagating the Gospel in all Pagan Countries', to raise funds to train clergy in pagan languages and send them out as missionaries, in his *Geographical Grammar*. Further proposals, designed for a later edition of the text, indicated that Gordon decided his first plan was impractical due to the multiplicity of indigenous languages. Instead, missionary schools should be established amongst Native American communities to teach them both English and Christianity.[172] Though Gordon's revised proposals proved too ambitious for the SPG to implement, they are indicative of the political and cultural imaginaries that shaped early colonial missionary endeavours. Gordon only survived for a few months after his arrival as a missionary in North America. He and George Keith travelled by ship together, and Keith writes warmly of that shared experience, so the proposals remain suggestive of a vision that framed how these two men conceptualised and enacted their role as the SPG's earliest missionaries. This example indicates how the SPG's mission was shaped from its inauguration by men with professional experience as geographers and surveyors. Keith's later manuscript journals, his reporting on the status of his work and travels via letter, and the broad dissemination of his published apologetics in favour of Anglicanism evidence a porous movement between manuscript and print and demonstrates how

---

[171] Gerbner, 'Antislavery in Print'; Ferlier, 'George Keith (1639–1716)'.
[172] SPG 7 4–7. Endorsed December 1701.

printed texts were indexed and distributed as objects of pastoral care via manuscript letters in a colonial space where the competition between different Christian groups for the allegiance of European settlers was fierce.

Keith's own very public conversion from Quaker apologist to Anglican missionary to the colonies can be partially understood in terms of his intellectual trajectory as a theologian: 'Keith viewed the theological status of 'outward-ness', especially as it related to the body of Christ', as more significant than the Philadelphian Quakers he disputed with considered it to be. This was a key aspect of 'Keith's intellectual journey . . . a shift which took him from the centre of Quakerism towards the margins, and, ultimately, out of the movement altogether'.[173] Madelaine Ward suggests that two further inferences can be drawn from Keith's experience. First, a positive evaluation of 'outwardness' meant that it was impossible to separate the physical from the spiritual, and this shaped a less complacent attitude amongst Keith's supporters to the institution of slavery than that evidenced by George Fox, contributing to 'the remarkably early disavowal of slavery issued by the Keithian Monthly Meeting at Philadelphia in 1693'.[174] Second, Keith's controversy with the Quakers in Philadelphia was part of the movement's coming of age, and shows how the balance of power between centre and periphery could be recalibrated: 'In the first instance . . . the dispute was aggravated by the low educational standards in the new colony', reflecting a model where 'Quaker leaders in London arranged for the distribution of educational literature; colonial Quakers received it'.[175] However, Pennsylvania 'was a relative haven compared to the fragile situation in England'[176] and this created a very different, and more hospitable, political environment for ecclesiological experimentation and theological debate.

Keith's adeptness at leveraging print resources, networks of power, and the gaps between the 'religious epicentre' and the establishment of a dependent community in the American colonies built on decades of experience as a formidable nonconformist controversialist.[177] Ironically, it was precisely these qualifications that made the SPG's decision to employ Keith as one of their first missionaries such a mutually satisfactory and productive relationship. The aspirations of the SPG to resource a wider transatlantic Anglican commu-nion replicated many aspects of developing Quaker networks in London and Pennsylvania, including navigating shifting balances of power between centre and periphery which were a consequence, in part, of significant variations in forms of local governance on the margins of European settlement. It is harder to sustain the claim that Keith's positive valorisation of 'outwardness' was an important influence on the development of anti-slavery sentiments, though his

---

[173] Ward, *The Christian Quaker.*   [174] Ibid.   [175] Ibid.   [176] Ibid.   [177] Ibid.

substantial experience of pamphlet production meant that he helped to arrange for the publication of the *Exhortation*. Katherine Gerbner argues that its 'anti-slavery ideology should be attributed to nonelite German, Dutch, Welsh, Irish, Scottish, and English Quakers who had been heavily influenced by the ideas introduced by the German-Dutch settlers in Germantown, Pennsylvania'.[178]

The final two parts of this section will examine the correspondence of Elias Neau, a catechist based in New York City, and Dr Francis Le Jau, a missionary-priest caring for a rural parish in North Carolina, with the SPG, which supported them both materially and pastorally in their vocations. This two-site focus offers comparative insights into the ways in which Anglican missionaries negotiated engagement with diverse communities in North America during the earliest years of the SPG's operations, and evidences the Society's emergence as a prominent religious patron on the eastern seaboard in the early decades of its corporate identity formation and experimentation with bureaucratic practices resulting in a powerful, coercive, and enabling network of transatlantic care administered largely through the exchange of letters.

Elias Neau: The SPG Catechist in New York

The correspondence of Elias Neau shows how the SPG navigated support and pastoral caregiving in an urban parish that involved complicated political negotiations between the colonial periphery and the metropolitan centre in the selection and allocation of resources, and the challenges resulting from the absence of a local bishop, leading to competing appeals to the Bishop of London and the SPG as alternative sources of authority and patronage for the receipt and provision of pastoral care. Neau's correspondence with the SPG during his period as a catechist to enslaved people in New York exposes other issues faced by the SPG's employees when giving and receiving pastoral care. Neau's French Huguenot background demonstrates the SPG's willingness to draw ecumenically on European Protestants to do missionary work in North America, despite the Anglican establishment's intense antipathy to English Protestant nonconformists in England, but letters by Neau and others in the SPG archive reveal the tensions that arose from these national and denominational differences, playing out particularly in terms of education, pedagogical methodologies, and proficiency in written English. These tensions expose anxieties around the construction of pastoral authority, its intersections with the establishment of the English state church in New York City and developing ideals of the English cleric as a gentleman of status. Neau's own experience of imprisonment for his Protestant religious convictions, conflicts resulting from

---

[178] Gerbner, 'Antislavery in Print', 554–5.

the incommensurability between the economic priorities of slave masters and the SPG's missionary imperative to catechise enslaved people and provide access to literacy and books, and how these factors shaped the politics of an urban parish struggling to resource and provide pastoral care to a diverse population can be traced in correspondence from 1703–6.

Neau presents himself as an ideal candidate for the role of SPG catechist to enslaved people in New York City. In line with Protestant tradition, he observes that he has an extensive collection of good books in French and English that will equip him to do such work well. He is also clearsighted about the systemic power structures shaping the environment in which he operates: laws need to be enacted; owners of enslaved people should be required to contribute to the spiritual care of those who underwrite their material prosperity; the catechists employed need to be proficient in multiple languages, free from other entanglements – especially in relation to enslaved people – and able to establish good relationships with ministers who can help to hold the catechists accountable.[179]

On 10 July 1703, Neau wrote to John Hodges, the SPG Treasurer, noting his willingness 'to follow the Calling, wherew[i]th the Illust[rious] Religious Society was willing to honor me', but suggesting that his inability to 'speak the Indian language' meant that it would be more useful to 'find out some methods' for the 'Instruction' of 'a great Number of Slaves w[hi]ch we Call \negroes/, of both Sexes & of all Ages ... & of whom \there is no manner of/ Care taken, 'tis a thing Worthy of the Charity of the Glorious Body of the Society, to Endeavor'.[180] Neau states that it would be useful if Parliament, or the General Assembly, would pass a law: 'w[hi]ch permitted the Inhabitants to \Cause/ their \negroes to be/ Instructed and Baptised ... provided \nevertheless/ that the slaves \might have/ no Right to Pretend to \a/ \Temporall/ Liberty, because \that/ would be \a/ great \Injury/ to \Plantations w[hi]ch are only supported/ by the \Labor/ of these People'. Otherwise, the 'Masters, viz, all the Inhabitants w[oul]d oppose it'.[181] The torturous formulation of this letter reveals not only the linguistic issues presented by cross-cultural mission and transatlantic communication but also the challenges created when attempting to negotiate the provision of pastoral care for enslaved human beings owned by others.[182] Neau argues that 'Every Master' should contribute to the salaries of '\such as/ w[oul]d take Care to Catechise them, for there should be sev[era]ll

---

[179] SPG 13 29.

[180] SPG 13 28–9. Dated 10 July 1703; French (28) with English translation (29).

[181] SPG 13 29.

[182] Baxter's casuistical critique of the Atlantic slave trade and the purchase of enslaved persons by European Christians in *The Christian Directory* (1673) demonstrates that responses to the development of slavery as an institution, and the distortions in pastoral care provision that it entailed, were diverse, even amongst Reformed Protestants:

Persons \fitt/ for that, \business both in Town & Country as well/ English, as Dutch & French'. He would like to see this 'great work' done throughout all the plantations, especially where he is based in New York.

Neau offers an illuminating vignette that clearly reveals the cultural, economic, and social entanglements that shaped the environment within which he sought to provide pastoral care:

> On Sundays, while we are at \our/ Devotions, the Streets are full of Negroes, who Dance & Divert themselves, for they are kept after the same Manner as horses, for to \gett from them/ all the Work \one/ Can, w[i]thout \any concern for/ their Salvation: Moreover, you ought not to \think it strange/, if I propose \that/ the Masters \be oblig'd/ to pay a Piece of Eight for \the Instruction of/ Each Negroe; Every thing is Extreamly Dear here, & they that have Negroes have wherew[i]thall to pay th[a]t but \those that are to Instruct them must be such as shall lay to heart the/ Glory of God, & \give themselves wholly to that Business/ for I believe betw[ee]n you & I, this Office can't be \perform'd by a Person who/, at the same time \should be taken up w[i]th/ \the Worldly Employm[en]ts of his Negros therefore there must be a handsom honestly allowed subsistence to the Catechists/ \the/ Ministers, who \also ought to/ Examin \from time to time/, what progress \they make/. .... I have God b[e] thanked, a great many fine & Good Books, English & French, so that if I am admitted into this Office, I shall have wherew[i]thall [to] Employ my self to \require/ new Lights in the [Chris]tian Religion, \&/ to \cause my neighbo[ur]s to p[ar]take/ thereof.[183]

However, even when catechist and minister agreed on the pastoral care required by youths and enslaved people in New York City,[184] the local politics of pastoral care and metropolitan patronage could prove challenging, as a letter from William Vesey, minister of Neau's parish, to the Bishop of London on 26 October 1704 makes clear. Neau and Vesey differ in their judgment as to who should meet the pastoral needs of the parish; this variance in opinion is communicated from the colonial peripheries of the church to overlapping but different authorities – the SPG's Secretary and Treasurer and the Bishop of London – at its centre. It is all done through letters: Vesey acknowledges that Neau 'has been a noble confessor' of Protestantism, 'of a most zealous

---

To go as Pirats and catch up poor *Negro's* or people of another Land, that never forfeited Life or Liberty, and to make them slaves, and sell them, is one of the worst kinds of Thievery in the world; and such persons are to be taken for the common enemies of mankind; And they that buy them and use them as beasts, for their meer commodity, and betray or destroy or neglect their souls, are fitter to be called incarnate Devils than Christians, though they be no Christians whom they so abuse (p. 559).

See further Norbrook, "A Fleet of Worlds".   [183] SPG 13 29.

[184] On urban populations in Britain and North America and their capacity to sustain local postal services and news publications see Steele, *The English Atlantic*, 132–67.

exemplary life & deserves singular respect', but Vesey also observes Neau is a lay elder of the French congregation, a merchant, and cannot speak good English. He is not a 'proper Assistant' for Vesey in his parish and appointing him to the office of catechist without ordination will 'prejudice the interest of the Church'.[185] Vesey was rector of Trinity Church, Manhattan, from 1697–1746, and played an instrumental role in establishing the Anglican church within New York City. This early correspondence, directed to the Bishop of London, rather than the Secretary or Treasurer of the SPG, demonstrates Vesey's concern with the reputation of the church above ecumenical or evangelical priorities and an emphasis on episcopal ordination. He suggests that the schoolmaster, George Muirson, would be a more strategic choice for the role of SPG catechist with its £50 per annum salary. Vesey does not dispute the authenticity of Neau's appointment, which he has seen confirmed in a letter, but he suggests that the SPG was misinformed about Neau: 'the Great End of the Society would be better served by Mr Muirson. And indeed My Lord there is a very great occasion of A Catechist in this City of New York here being a great number of youths & and of Negro & Indian slaves that need Instruction and I am no longer able to performe all offices without an Assistant'.[186] Vesey requests that Muirson be appointed as catechist and assistant to him, with a salary of £50, which he will supplement with £30 from his own income should Muirson help him in all offices, submitting this 'to your Lord[shi]ps judgment & care'.[187]

Vesey and Neau's letters with competing accounts and requests, and Muirson himself en route to England to receive episcopal ordination, and bearing a letter from Lord Cornbury, all travelled from the eastern seaboard of America in the latter part of 1704.[188] Neau's account of the political, linguistic, and ecclesiological matters shaping his pastoral practices as the SPG's catechist offers a different vision of the parish to that provided by Vesey. Neau affirms his commitment to the English church and liturgy, despite the misunderstanding of others in the French community. However, he refuses to condemn those who do not conform to the English state church, despite emphasising that he cannot be accused 'of being a Dissenter' himself. Neau establishes a different genealogy

---

[185] SPG 13 85. Dated 26 October 1704. This item is catalogued as addressed to Thomas Tenison, Archbishop of Canterbury, but this appears to conflate the cover of SPG 13 84 with 85. The issues Vesey raises fall under the jurisdiction of the Bishop of London, Henry Compton. In a letter sent to Chamberlayne two days later (SPG 13 91), Vesey notes: 'I am im[m]ediately under the jurisdiction of My L[or]d B[isho]p of London & to him accountable for all my management and therefore in obedience to His Lord[shi]p dare not countenance any person in my Parish as an officer of the Church ... until ordain'd or licensed by His Lordship'.

[186] SPG 13 85.   [187] Ibid.

[188] SPG 13 85; SPG 13 101–2. In SPG 13 96 Lord Cornbury notes that his letter is carried by Muirson who 'is able' to give Chamberlayne 'very good accounts of all matters here'. Cf. also SPG 13 100.

of authority to that of episcopal ordination: his period of imprisonment for commitment to Protestantism. Neau developed his knowledge of, and affection for, the state church liturgy from an English Bible smuggled to him while incarcerated in a dungeon. Neau astutely deploys a rhetoric of epistolary self-fashioning that he knows will resonate with the SPG and its mission, implicitly arguing that his experience and suffering render him a more appropriate candidate for the pastoral care of youths and enslaved persons in the mixed population of New York than an ordained English priest.[189]

Neau constructs himself as a disinterested pastor capable of appealing to and caring for the diverse communities he seeks to convert and catechise, loyal to the SPG, rather than the parish priest, as his primary patron. Neau observes that the minister of the parish (i.e. Vesey) is hindering him from pursuing the 'Catechumen Slaves', and that though:

> Mr G. Muirson went hence w[i]th the Man of War in Order to be Ordained & have the Office of Catechist w[i]th the Approbation of Mr Vesey our Pastor. I believe he is a very Honest Man, but I am Affraid the Good Opinion People have of him will be lost before he comes back, & I have some new reasons to confirm My former suspicion thereof.[190]

This is clinched in the postscript, where Neau notes that given the more vulnerable position of the state church in colonial America, it is necessary for Muirson to have the favour of the people, 'or it will cause a great deal of Trouble in Mr V:'s Ch[urc]h. He seems already not to have it much'.[191] Neau concludes: 'As for me I am Resolved to do all the Service I can to t[h]e Illustrious Society w[i]thout p[re]tending to Eccles[iastica]l Hon[ou]rs'.[192]

Neau's letter to John Chamberlayne a year later indicates that his epistolary self-fashioning and negotiation were effective. He expresses appreciation for: 'The Letter that [Chamberlayne] Charit[a]bly \took the pains/ to write', which confirmed him in the office of SPG catechist. Mr Vesey had received a letter to the same effect from the Bishop of London. Together they waited on Lord Cornbury, who confirmed the licence that he had already given Neau. Epistolary authorisation from the metropolitan centre was critical and had immediate practical effect: 'Mr Vesey ... read a note on Sunday morning in the Church in form of an exhortation to the masters and mistresses to take care \to/ send me their slaves every Wednesday Friday and Sunday at Five a Clock in the Evening'.[193] However, Neau's assessment of the effectiveness of his pastoral

---

[189] SPG 13 101–2. Dated 20 December 1704; French (102) with English translation (101).
[190] SPG 13 101. See also SPG 13 111–3.   [191] SPG 13 101.   [192] Ibid.
[193] SPG 13 135–6. Dated 3 October 1705; French (136) with English translation (135). There are also copies of later letters that Chamberlayne sent to Neau (in French) and Vesey (in English) on 3 May 1706.

care work catechising enslaved persons was attenuated. He stringently critiques the morals of slave masters: they neither take to heart their own salvation, nor do they care for the salvation of those they enslave. Neau recognises that 'the trouble \which/ the Gentleman of the illustrious Society give themselves for those people as well as for the Indians' could prove to be unsuccessful despite his best endeavours. Mr Vesey has promised to preach a sermon to stir up some zeal in 'the masters for their Slaves'.[194] Accompanying his letter is a list of those 'that have sent me their Blacks to Catechise, and to whom I have given Catechisms and other good Books'. The names of slave-owners, starting with Cornbury and Vesey, and the number of catechisms and books are itemised; enslaved people are listed in numbers, identified only by gender and colour/ ethnicity, following the name of their master or mistress.[195]

Neau chooses to send his letter by way of Boston, as he fears the fleet then in New York will not sail that winter. Regular updates to the metropolitan centre were essential: the SPG expected them, and Neau's financial and pastoral authority depended on the SPG's ongoing support. However, Neau is honest when evaluating the viability of funding the role of catechist to enslaved persons within hierarchical structures that actively demotivated those who owned enslaved people from supporting their spiritual care and instruction, particularly beyond a session on Sunday: 'these people come in \such/ great numbers' (as his enclosed list enumerates) 'Sundays \only/, Wednesdays & Fridays there comes but eight or ten some times more and some times less'.[196] Neau concludes that he has a 'prety good \understanding/ with Mr Vesey now', but also that he will 'write ... faithfully what \effect/ the \Employ/ of Catechist will produce \I hope to know by a real experience/ and \whether it/ deserves \to take up a mans time/'.[197] Neau was a successful merchant and businessman. He is evaluating the effectiveness of his engagement in pastoral care to enslaved persons by a pragmatic standard that is his own, as much as it might be imposed by the bureaucratic structures of the SPG, to whom he sends his epistolary accounts. This is, to some extent, cemented by his concluding observation on the disadvantage which episcopal ordination would be to his effectiveness as an SPG catechist: 'I think my self obliged also to tell you that I shall \be more serviceable/ without taking orders than if I tooke them because it will seem less affect\ed/'.[198]

---

[194] SPG 13 135.
[195] SPG 13 138–9; list in French (138) with English translation (139). On a subsequent list, Neau notes: 'It is impossible for me to keep Count of the small Books that I distribute, for I give them equally to the whites & Blacks and I kept this account only to prove my Sincerity in disposing of the good Books that the illustrious Society sent me.' SPG 13 170.
[196] SPG 13 135.   [197] Ibid. See also SPG 13 174.
[198] SPG 13 135. SPG 13 190: Minutes regarding Neau note he has received a licence from the Bishop of London to catechise and to teach a school.

Neau's letter to Chamberlayne on 30 April 1706, brings into focus the challenges presented by a mixed history of European colonisation and urban versus rural communities. Most fundamental, however, is the incommensurability of owning other humans for one's material benefit, whilst acknowledging accountability for their souls. As Neau states, this tension jeopardises the SPG's project to convert enslaved people through catechesis:[199]

> I Continue to Ca=techise all the Slaves that are sent to me, Mr Vesey has baptiz'd some against the Will and without the knowledge of their Masters, be=cause they \fear/ \lest/ by baptism they should become \temporally/ free, \both Mr Vesey & I/ have said all we could on that Subject, to encourage their Masters, especially the Dutch and French, but we cannot free them from their fear, so that, we are resolved S[i]r to do all we can, for to Obtain an Act of Assembly, to Confirm the right of the Inhabitants over their slaves after Baptism, in the same manner that they had it before, for w[i]th out that, they will not suffer them to be Ins=tructed, for fear they should be baptiz'd w[i]th out their knowledge.[200]

Neau identifies the need for legislation to require owners of enslaved persons to commit to caring for the souls as well as the bodies of those who worked for them in both agricultural and domestic spaces; he also articulated this in an earlier letter to Hodges. Neau did not question the structure of slavery that underwrote his own financial security and social position, but he had no sympathy for slave masters who refused to facilitate the Christian catechising and education of the people they owned due to selfishness, indifference, or fear. Evangelistic passion was powerful but limited in its capacity to engineer social change. Indeed, it resulted in legislation that constrained the agency of enslaved Africans even further. This was the ultimate outcome of Neau's sedulous attempts to persuade masters to allow enslaved people to be catechised in the Christian religion on the premise that conversion would not result in manumission.[201]

Francis Le Jau: SPG Missionary-Priest in South Carolina

Annette Laing argues that the first fifteen years of the SPG's mission work in South Carolina can be differentiated from what followed suggesting that the social position of missionaries 'at the fringe of the Atlantic world was steeped in both fierce ambition and deep insecurity'. Over time, as white settlers showed themselves 'ecumenical in outlook' and the white elite became 'increasingly well-defined and invested in the practice of conspicuous gentility', missionary

---

[199] SPG 13 201–2. Dated 30 April 1706; French (202) with English translation (201).
[200] SPG 13 201. See also SPG 13 236. [201] Gerbner, *Christian Slavery*, 196.

insecurity grew.[202] Missionaries were split between dependence on the approval of the SPG and the goodwill of planter neighbours for their professional survival and personal status. This meant their pastoral authority, financial stability, and the boundaries of their congregation and parish, including their competing responsibilities to white settlers, enslaved Africans, and Native Americans were fluid and contingent: 'Often disadvantaged by their ethnic or provincial origins', such clergy joined the SPG in hope of 'securing more remunerative and respectable careers in America. They expected to enjoy amply furnished parsonages, comfortable incomes, and the deference of their parishioners'.[203] This forms a strong contrast to Matthew Hill's correspondence with Richard Baxter discussed earlier. A nonconformist immigrant to Maryland in the late seventeenth century, Hill demonstrates a similar indigency, but quite different expectations regarding deference and financial security in return for providing pastoral care. The clergy, in each instance, are shown to be dependent on a resource base in England organised via letters for pastoral care and provision. However, nonconformists of varying sects assume a different guise when refracted through the lens of Anglicanism as colonial missionaries reported back in letters on their pastoral work.

Dr Francis Le Jau, one of the earliest Anglican missionaries to work for the SPG in South Carolina, provides an informative counterpoint to the work of Neau as an SPG catechist in New York. Le Jau was assigned a rural, rather than urban, parish, and worked as a missionary-priest, caring for French as well as English settlers. As one of the most regular and fulsome correspondents with the SPG Secretary, Le Jau's letters provide valuable insight into how epistolary reporting and exchange could work across the British Atlantic, encompassing matters of intellectual and emotional as well as parochial interest and care. Letters between the SPG and early missionaries such as Le Jau, and missionaries corresponding with one another, offer an insight into how the SPG became a patron of pastoral care provision on the eastern seaboard, the ways missionaries attempted to define, understand, and implement their role as providers of pastoral care in situations of geographical and cultural entanglement, and the competition between missionaries for resources from London to provide for themselves and their families, and to exercise pastoral care and power effectively. Here, as Vesey and Neau discovered in New York, the absence of bishops in North America confronted Anglican ministers with issues of authority and guidance that were not shared by their nonconformist neighbours and posed challenges in ecumenical settler zones when attempting to establish parish structures and new forms of pastoral care. Somewhat ironically, this meant

---

[202] Laing, '"Heathens and Infidels"?' 216.   [203] Ibid. 204.

that the SPG's missionaries raised casuistical issues, including challenges to administering the sacraments, that were like those confronted by Protestant nonconformists in England after the Restoration.

Le Jau (1665–1717), originally a French Huguenot, but educated at Trinity College, Dublin, arrived in South Carolina in 1706 after spending some time on the island of St Christopher. His surviving letters to the SPG in London reveal the precariousness of European settlement and a new transatlantic community of care during its contingent formation. From a letter Le Jau sent to the SPG early in 1717, it appears that the centralisation of this epistolary network in London, under the control of the Secretary, was a matter of both protocol and control, as Le Jau apologised for writing to other SPG members, rather than to the Secretary.[204] Structures of accountability and reporting back to the centre discipline the epistolary narration of community life revealing how bureaucratic processes colonise care by privileging certain ways of thinking about bodies and knowledges. This requirement for epistolary accountability created anxiety on the part of conscientious missionaries, particularly given the tenuous logistics of communication structures transporting letters and packets across the Atlantic in the early eighteenth century. Six years earlier, Le Jau noted in a letter that besides the one he hopes will come to the Secretary's hands from the Post Office (where he gives an account of his mission), he plans to send his current letter and other papers via the wife of his fellow missionary, Gideon Johnston. In addition, Le Jau has given several letters to Captain Cole – 'I should be sorry if they were lost' – as well as sending a letter via Barbados and some more via Captain Belcher.[205]

The frequency of Le Jau's correspondence with the SPG from 1706–17, resulting from his relatively settled status as a missionary in South Carolina, means his developing practices of pastoral care can be examined in detail. Le Jau's scrupulous attention to epistolary accountability is revealed in a letter 'a board the Greenwich In the Queens dock near Plimouth', where he addresses the Secretary, Chamberlayne, to acquaint him with a delay in the departure of his ship due to foul winds and subsequent damage:

> I hear our head was worm eaten else it would not have been so easily broke and I believe this Accident has happen'd through God's mercy that the ship may be made safer . . .. I won't fail to let you know how things are in relation

---

[204] SPG Series A12, 73–76. Dated 19 January 1717. The spiritual account that Le Jau gives of his parish in this letter from 1 July–31 December 1716 reflects the information that the SPG required its missionaries to send every six months as set out in a standard *Notitia Parochialis* form (see Glasson, *Mastering Christianity*, 36).

[205] SPG 17 36–7. Dated 12 April 1711.

to my going That The honourable Society my Superiors and Worthy bene-
factors may be Informed of it.[206]

In a subsequent letter dated 2 December 1706, Le Jau reports his safe arrival in
South Carolina via Virginia in October. He provides Chamberlayne with an
update on other clergy: Samuel Thomas died ten days before he arrived and is
'universal\ly/ Lamented by all good Men'; another 'Brother ... has thought fit
to stay in Bermudas where I suppose a Minister was wanting. Mr Dunn has been
afflicted with the feaver and Ague, and as he was on the recovery is fallen sick
again, & continues so still'.[207] However, Le Jau gives a positive account of the
reception he received from local notables, learned people, and 'even from the
dissenters I have seen'. Due to 'the sickness which was still raging in town', he
was 'carryd to the Country in the Parish The Society was pleasd to give me the
care of'.[208]

Le Jau's view on life in South Carolina and his parish shifted significantly as
he became more experienced, but his initial assessment was optimistic:

> The change of Climate & The fatigue of my voyage had somewhat disordered
> my health. Through Gods blessing I am pretty well for the present; and when
> I am season'd to the Country I hope Ill do well. Our Church and Parsonage
> house will be fitted up in a short time. Materials are getting ready very fast. In
> the mean time great & Charitable care is taken of me att Mr Moore's .... I am
> the more Particular on this account because I think it an Act of Justice to
> undeceive the world; and Let such Clergy men as the Society please to send
> come freely they will find matters as I say, & much better; for I must own that
> for gentility Politeness and a handsome way of living this Colony exceeds
> what I have seen. Poor familyes may come here, and will live very well ....[209]

Le Jau is confident that when he is 'season'd' to the country, his health will be
better, and that the civility, ease, and prosperity of the region provide a viable
settlement opportunity for both clergy and poor (British) Christians. Le Jau also
provides a brief description of his parish's demographic: 'there is 100 familyes
in my parish. few dissenters & several Negroes come to Church', but notes that
he 'will tell the particulars ... according to the form prescribed in the
Instructions; in a little time: for I am in a manner unsettled yet'.[210] His
inexperience, however, does not prevent him from actively assessing opportunities for evangelistic outreach to Native Americans, and he provides a detailed
plan that he hopes will achieve this. The copy of the letter sent by the Secretary
to Le Jau on 17 May 1707 acknowledges his positive account of the country but

---

[206] SPG 16 112–3. Dated 6 May 1706.   [207] SPG 16 141–3. Dated 2 December 1706.
[208] Ibid.   [209] Ibid.
[210] Ibid. Le Jau notes that: 'our poor people & Negroes ... had a share in the distribution of the
small tracts'. Ibid.

resists the idea of a mission to Native Americans due to the difficulties the SPG had faced in New York. However, real concern and an acknowledgement of duty of care is expressed for Samuel Thomas's family: 'his Poor Wife & Family wil long feel this severe Providence, God comfort them and I hope our society wil do some=thing towards wiping the Tears from their Eyes'.[211]

A subsequent letter to Philip Stubbs, the rector of St Alphage, Cripplegate, London, some nine months later, reveals that Le Jau's wife and children have joined him in South Carolina. The letter thanks Stubbs for his 'readiness full of Charity to do service to my family in my absence'.[212] It also reveals the health challenges that missionary families faced when travelling. They arrived in July: 'a sickly time with New comers by reason of the heat which lasts about three Months. my children have been sick of the feaver and through the mercy of God they are now pretty well recoverd. my wife is still very much out of order, but I hope she will conquer it'.[213] Le Jau also presents brief cameos of two women in this letter that reveal some of the difficulties he faced when seeking to develop practices of pastoral care in his parish in South Carolina: 'the woman accused of witchcraft has sometime been set at liberty, but is presently confined again by reason of new mischiefs she dos'. Though now imprisoned, 'she boasts of the number of friends she has and says she will come off'.[214] This account follows Le Jau's more general observations about 'malecontents' and 'dissenters', rendering the issues of gender disorderliness, spiritual discipline, and law enforcement that he is seeking to navigate in concrete detail.

Le Jau then offers a longer description of 'a Pious woman \who/ lived in my parish with her husband and family', which indicates the sense of responsibility he feels for everyone within the parameters of the parish of St James. The woman's sickness was followed by 'a raving condition for 3 weeks', but she then came to herself for six hours:

> she being in her right mind declared that she had been dead and told several surprising particulars of what she had seen and heard and was not at all sensible that she had been raving. having spoken rationally for those 6 hours she lost her strength and senses and dyed 2 days after I buryd her a month ago. she desired me when she was in her right mind to Instruct the Company att her funeral taking my subject from Job.19.25&c I know that my Redeemer liveth &c.[215]

Le Jau is very careful here to navigate between his parishioner's rationality and raving: he emphasises the important point that she dies well and was, when 'in her right mind', able to instruct him as to how to edify the company at her funeral. This rite of service, which Le Jau conducts as the parish clergyman,

---

[211] SPG 16 157–8.   [212] SPG 16 178. Dated 23 September 1707.   [213] Ibid.   [214] Ibid.
[215] Ibid.

ceremonially frames the conundrums this woman's physical and mental health present and helps to underwrite Le Jau's pastoral authority: 'I must say of her she was the most resigned soul to the will of God, both in her health and sickness that I saw in this Country, she was bred among a sort of Anabaptists & knew no better till of late'.[216]

Le Jau then shifts to a broader appraisal of the intractability of nonconformists and the implications for his role as an Anglican missionary in South Carolina. The Anabaptists have 'a New teacher a brick layer by trade who is joined to an old Carpenter'.[217] He clearly conceptualises his role as involving responsibility for the whole parish, but the settled position of nonconformists in South Carolina means that negotiating the boundaries of salvation and 'our church' is a more ambivalent act of pastoral care and engagement than it was within an English parish, such as that administered by Le Jau's correspondent, Stubbs. Through the epistolary act of writing to a clerical peer, Le Jau attempts to inscribe order on human diversity and render the shape of his role legible to himself and to his interlocutor:

> It is grievous to see poor souls thus deluded. those among them who have a true desire to serve God and be saved come to our church. as for the others who mind nothing but this worlds happiness I pray for them, for I find it is needless to talk to them of Jesus Ch[rist] their heart being fixd up[on a]n outward appearance of reformation and fine words. if they could get money by coming to [ours] I don't believe there would be a dissenter here. be pleased to honour me with the Continuance of your friendship.[218]

The continuance of friendship nourished through the exchange of letters is crucial to Le Jau's own well-being. He asks for Stubbs's prayers, and notes that the SPG Treasurer, 'Mr hodges will be so kind as to send me your letters'.[219] Even personal correspondence between friends is directed through the central administrative channels of the SPG to ensure that it reaches missionaries at the peripheries of European settlement in North America.

Le Jau's letter to the SPG Secretary, Chamberlayne, a year later reveals how the contingent, entangled histories of rural parishes such as his created spaces for experimentation that shaped colonising practices of pastoral care on the eastern seaboard.[220] As an Anglican missionary-priest in South Carolina, Le Jau's role was to set up a parish modelled on the English system. The letter was written on 15 September, 1708, several years after he was first appointed and reveals the continuing dependence of missionaries in settler communities upon the SPG's financial resources and support. Le Jau's parsonage is unfinished, the

---

[216] Ibid.   [217] Ibid.   [218] Ibid.   [219] Ibid.
[220] SPG 16 224–5. Francis Le Jau to John Chamberlayne, 15 September 1708.

statute designed to provide support for ministers is ineffective, and the promises made to him when he sent for his family and resigned his minor canonship have not been kept. Le Jau is experiencing long-term sickness in an uncongenial climate, and this interrupts his pastoral labours, but also opens an opportunity for reciprocal caregiving. He notes: 'My Parishioners have Comforted and assisted me very much during my sickness'.[221] Le Jau's report to the SPG's Secretary as to the spiritual state of his parish reveal how modes of evaluation and accountability imposed at the centre structure his epistolary narrative,[222] as he admits: 'I am onely sorry the number is so small. there is no great addition to the spiritual state of this Parish since my last Letters'.[223]

The local context Le Jau depicts, however, is not simply a poor rural parish made up of white European settlers. His epistolary interlocutor is keenly interested in indigenous languages and how they might be utilised to spread scripture, in this case the Lord's Prayer is given as an example. Le Jau's reflections on settler engagement with Native Americans reveal the incommensurability between trading, educational, and evangelising endeavours. Dissolute Europeans trade with Native Americans and deliberately provoke war to create a market for their goods and to obtain slaves in return. Le Jau notes that this 'is a great obstruction to our best designs', presumably a reference to missionary aims to convert Native Americans through a combination of assimilation and education.[224] The complicity of the situation in which he is also implicated becomes clear as he observes: 'the slaves We have for Necessary service, for our white servants in a months time prove good for nothing at all'.[225] Several years later Le Jau himself had purchased three enslaved people in order to maintain his own frugal household demonstrating an increasing and (to him) unavoidable investment as a missionary-priest in the processes of colonisation and enslavement.[226]

Such entanglements also presented casuistical difficulties for the European missionary attempting to provide pastoral care to the souls of Native Americans, enslaved people, white servants, and white masters within the same parish.[227] Le Jau refers one such scruple to the 'Hon[oura]ble Society'

---

[221] Ibid.

[222] The intimate and violent connections between imperial modes of accounting, the aesthetics of orderly paperwork, and their intergenerational legacies are incisively interrogated by Carby, *Imperial Intimacies*, 243–54.

[223] SPG 16 224–5.

[224] Ibid. See also the undated proposal of SPG missionary Samuel Thomas, who died just before Le Jau arrived in South Carolina, that included suggestions for the instruction of Native Americans and enslaved Africans. SPG 17 80–7.

[225] SPG 16 224–5. See also Chakravarty, *Fictions of Consent*.

[226] Francis Le Jau to John Chamberlayne, 12 April 1711. SPG 17 36–7.

[227] SPG 8 72. A letter from the Bishop of London to Chamberlayne commenting on the SPG's minutes mentions that Le Jau also undertook to care for the French colony adjacent to his parish.

for adjudication: 'whether or no we are to Answer for grievous sins dayly committed by all our slaves here and elsewhere, and tolerated or at least connived at by us under a pretence of Impossibility to Remedy Them'.[228] Le Jau is certain that a reformation of manners would be possible amongst the enslaved population if more of an effort were made, but masters care only about getting as much labour as possible from the human beings they own and are unconcerned about habits of promiscuous cohabitation. Le Jau's role as a missionary-priest reveals the social and logistical fissures that emerge when attempting to provide spiritual care for people who are categorised as property objectified to enhance the material well-being and profit of others. This created distinct challenges for ministers formulating practices of spiritual care at a moment when white settler societies were insecurely established, and the full apparatus of colonisation, of which pastoral care was one component, was still being developed.

As Neau discovered in urban New York, Le Jau found as he settled into his ministry that one of the most contentious aspects of pastoral caregiving in a society materially dependent on unfree labour for its survival was the unpredictable power dynamics inherent within promoting the literacy and education of enslaved people as a key component of the conversion process. Le Jau's experience of working with enslaved catechumens led him to consider 'oral instruction as more amenable to masters and more suited to the conditions of enslaved people. This meant one of the keystones of missionary Anglicanism's religious program was eroded by contact with Atlantic slavery'.[229] Le Jau's close witnessing of the ways in which biblical texts, particularly the prophetic and eschatological parts, could be interpreted by enslaved people to promote resistance and self-assertion led him to modify his practices of pastoral care.[230] But distance and the very different conditions of his rural parish in South Carolina to either urban or rural parishes in England meant that these changing practices of pastoral care had to be communicated with discretion to the SPG in London via letter. Le Jau wrote to the Secretary on 1 February 1710:

> I fear that those Men have not judgment enough to make a good use of their Learning; and I have thought most convenient not to urge too far that Indians and Negroes shou'd be indifferently admitted to learn to read, but I leave it to the discretion of their Masters whom I exhort to examine well their Inclinations. I have often observed and lately hear that it had been better if persons of a Melancholy Constitution or those that run into the Search after

---

He requested some French Books of Common Prayer and other titles fit to share amongst the French colonists whom he notes are well inclined and tractable.
[228] SPG 16 224–5.   [229] Glasson, *Mastering Christianity*, 109.   [230] Ibid. 108–9.

Curious matter had never seen a Book: pardon me if I disclose my thoughts
with too much freedome.[231]

Such modifications in pastoral care had long-term implications demonstrating
the problematic reach of pastoral power. Le Jau's response to an enslaved
person's astute and visionary interpretation of biblical prophecy highlights, as
Koritha Mitchell demonstrates, the importance of 'reading practices that center
success and recognize that marginalized groups pursue their definitions of
success much more than they respond to the violence they encounter; *violence
pursues them* because they accumulate achievements. . . .'[232] As Le Jau reports
to the Secretary, he 'took care to undeceive those who asked me about it'.[233]

    Several years of experience as a missionary-priest for the SPG in South
Carolina seasoned Le Jau beyond adjustment to the climate and the sicknesses
commonly attributed to it. The optimistic epistolary account he sent to
Chamberlayne after first arriving in December 1706 forms a stark contrast to
the 'melancholy narrative' he writes to the same recipient five years later:

> If the Society thinks fit to send any missionary to \any/ one of our vacant
> Parishes and they \should/ have familyes, if they be your friends I must
> Ingenuously declare they must prepare to suffer great hardships and
> Crosses. our poor Brother wood perishd of meer misery. Batchelors do well
> Enough if they be young and healthy. the poor man was some-what Elderly
> and broken & no care was taken of him. I make very hard shifts in my family,
> I have little or no help from my Parishioners who have much ado to maintain
> themselves we hardly have a joint of fresh meat once a week. Indian corn
> bread & water is the common food and drink for my children with a little milk
> sometimes, and to keep our house a little in order, which would be the work of
> one maid in England, is that of 3 Slaves which I have been forced to purchase
> by degrees, new and raw, and they are not wholly payd for yet. this melan-
> choly narrative is not all I suffer here.[234]

Le Jau invokes the concept of friendship as a standard by which the SPG should
evaluate their choice of missionaries, particularly if they have families. Even
bachelors need to be 'young and healthy', as those who are older can be 'broken'
because 'no care was taken'. This suggests an implicit critique of the SPG's
selection and appointment process when considering candidates for 'vacant
Parishes'.[235] These concerns were shared by Henry Compton, the Bishop of
London, who was responsible for identifying many of the candidates recommended as SPG missionaries. Compton's correspondence with Chamberlayne,
and his advice to the SPG committee, demonstrates a repeated concern that

---

[231] Cited in Ibid. 108–9.
[232] Mitchell, 'Identifying White Mediocrity and Know-Your-Place Aggression', 253.
[233] Glasson, *Mastering Christianity*, 108.   [234] SPG 17 36–7.   [235] Ibid.

candidates be appointed to an appropriate parish, and that nothing be done to discourage or dishearten them further, as the difficulty of the labour, and the frequent insecurity of the settler communities within which they served would prevent good men coming forward, and prompt those who were serving to leave their posts.[236]

Le Jau's vivid portrait of his own domestic situation illuminates the fragile material infrastructure that underwrites his capacity to provide pastoral care to the parish of St James and shows the ongoing dependence of the SPG's missionaries on financial support from the metropolitan centre. It also indicates that while Le Jau's pastoral practices were transformed through engagement with enslaved people's reading of scripture, he continued to assess his own status, role, and comfort in comparison with the experience of clerical peers in English parishes. His parishioners can provide very little help, as they are struggling 'to maintain themselves'. His children live mostly on cornbread and water; milk and fresh meat are relatively rare luxuries. In terms of domestic management, 'to keep our house a little in order', he has been required to purchase three slaves 'new and raw', to do the work that 'one maid in England' would have done.[237] Le Jau's epistolary reflections demonstrate how the SPG's attempts to set up pastoral caregiving on an English parish model exposed the incommensurable material and spiritual goals at the heart of the missionary project in settler communities in South Carolina in the early eighteenth century. The bureaucratic requirement imposed by the SPG that its missionaries report back regularly via letter to the Secretary on the progress of their work, and the absence of an episcopal authority within the American colonies, meant that these epistolary accounts of pastoral caregiving in liminal zones also challenged, unsettled, and expanded understandings of what constituted a parish and how parishes on the peripheries of empire should be supported by the metropolitan centre.[238] In practical terms this entailed grappling with, and debating through epistolary exchanges, who was an appropriate object of care; the power dynamics inherent within caregiving; the ways in which material and spiritual care intersect; how care should (or should not) be extended across different geographical contexts and worldviews; and the contestation of what constitutes care both between different caregivers as well as between the caregiver and the designated object of care.

---

[236] See, for example, SPG 8 14 and 8 78.　　[237] SPG 17 36–7.

[238] In a copy of his letter to Le Jau (SPG 17 235–6), the Secretary reassures him that 'you have equal'd if not exceeded any of the relations that have come from [the SPG's] other missionaries'. Dated 24 January 1708/9.

Conclusion

The exclusion of Protestant nonconformists from the post-Restoration English state church and the expansion of that church's reach beyond the parochial structure of a small nation-state into liminal geographical zones across the Atlantic created the opportunity and necessity for ecclesial experimentation in forms of pastoral care that could only be provided through the material technology of the letter. Pastoral care brings questions of agency, power, vulnerability, reciprocity, and the politics of caregiving into sharp focus. Letters, as a textual technology enabling communication and as a literary genre shaping intellect and emotion, entangle bodies, objects, and ideas in complex networks of exchange. In both the case studies examined here, letters do the paperwork that facilitates and resources pastoral care, often acting as an index to other objects (books, people, commodities), or as a prosthetic, enacting forms of literary cure and allowing the communion of saints to be imagined as a virtual community transcending some of the limitations of space and time. Following a small part of the paper trail left by two archives, *Pastoral Care Through Letters in the British Atlantic* explores several historical, political, and theological factors shaping the evolution of literary caregiving as a transatlantic Protestant textual practice between c. 1650 and 1720. These two case studies, and multiple others, could be reconstructed in various ways. Pastoral care is shadowed by pastoral power and its counter-conducts. Theological pedagogy welded to colonial exploitation produces at best a benign paternalism that cloaks, but cannot ameliorate, the violence that makes settler communities tenable.

Assessing pastoral care provision through letters foregrounds the critical and conflicted ways in which relationships between the material and spiritual were constructed in the early modern British Atlantic, and the limits this placed on the forms of communion and exchange that could be imagined. Enslavement irrevocably shaped eschatology and rendered a resurrected black body unimaginable for some early modern Protestant clerics and their parishioners.[239] As Le Jau notes, a woman asked him: 'Is it possible that any of my slaves could go to heaven, & must I see them there?' Incorporating enslaved people into shared religious communion involved a levelling that was construed as unacceptably radical in the present, and unimaginable in the future.[240] Yet, other options were imaginable. Richard Baxter utilised an inversion of the same eschatological calculus, relativising the present (and material) in the light of an anticipated (spiritual) future, in his casuistical denunciation of white Protestant European trade in black African bodies for temporal

---

[239] Trigg, 'The Racial Politics of Resurrection'.   [240] Glasson, *Mastering Christianity*, 89.

commercial profit: 'It is their heynous sin to buy them, unless it be in charity to deliver them . . . Having done it, undoubtedly they are presently bound to deliver them: Because by right the man is his own, and therefore no man else can have just title to him'.[241] The 'refusal to sequester past and present' is necessary to call 'into view what stands in slavery's wake', to free up 'futures is vital and necessary work that is bound up in how we fashion histories of the present that continually unsettle the past'.[242] I offer here a microhistory of pastoral caregiving through letters: it demonstrates the complicit and complex porosities between present and past, and the need for revolutionary imaginaries to reshape the politics of care. Letters have power to remake worlds.

---

[241] Baxter, *Christian Directory*, 559.   [242] Perry, 'Black Futures Not Yet Lost', 545, 557.

Bibliography

Manuscripts

Richard Baxter's Letters and Treatises. Dr Williams's Library.

The Society for the Propagation of the Gospel in Foreign Parts, Vols 7, 8 13, 16 & 17. Lambeth Palace Library.

The Society for the Propagation of the Gospel in Foreign Parts, Series A, Vol. 12. Bodleian Library.

Print Sources

Anselment, R. A. 'Robert Boyle and the Art of Occasional Meditation', *Renaissance and Reformation* 32.4 (2009), 73–92.

Archbold, W. A. J. & Cowie, L. W. 'Humphreys, David (1690–1740), Church of England Clergyman'. *Oxford Dictionary of National Biography*. 23 September 2004.

Arthur, E. 'The Future of Mission Agencies', *Mission Round Table* 12.1 (2017), 4–12.

Ballantyne, T., Paterson, L. & Wanhalla, A., eds., *Indigenous Textual Cultures: Reading and Writing in the Age of Global Empire*, Durham: Duke University Press, 2020.

Baxter, R. *The Christian Directory*, London, 1673.

Baxter, R. *The Cure of Church Divisions*, London, 1670.

Baxter, R. *Gildas Salvianus: The Reformed Pastor*, London, 1656.

Bingham, M. C. 'English Radical Religion and the Invention of the General Baptists, 1609–1660', *The Seventeenth Century* 34.4 (2019), 469–91.

Black, J. W. *Reformation Pastors: Richard Baxter and the Ideal of the Reformed Pastor*, Carlisle: Paternoster, 2004.

Brant, C. *Eighteenth-Century Letters and British Culture*, Houndmills: Palgrave Macmillan, 2006.

Bross, K. *Future History: Global Fantasies in Seventeenth-Century American and British Writings*, Oxford: Oxford University Press, 2017.

Bunting, M. *Labours of Love: The Crisis of Care*, London: Granta, 2020.

Burton, J. D. 'Crimson Missionaries: The Robert Boyle Legacy and Harvard College', *The New England Quarterly* 67.1 (1994), 132–40.

Carby, H. V. *Imperial Intimacies: A Tale of Two Islands*, London: Verso, 2019.

Chakravarty, U. *Fictions of Consent: Slavery, Servitude, and Free Service in Early Modern England*, Philadelphia: University of Pennsylvania Press, 2022.

Coffey, J. *John Goodwin and the Puritan Revolution: Religion and Intellectual Change in Seventeenth-Century England*, Woodbridge: Boydell & Brewer, 2006.

Cooper, T. 'Polity and Peacemaking: To What Extent Was Richard Baxter a Congregationalist?', E. Vernon & H. Powell, eds., *Church Polity and Politics in the British Atlantic World, c. 1635–66*, Manchester: Manchester University Press, 2020, 200–21.

Cooper, T. 'Richard Baxter and His Physicians', *Social History of Medicine* 20.1 (2007), 1–19.

Davies, M. 'Spirit in the Letters: John Bunyan's Congregational Epistles', *The Seventeenth Century* 24 (2009), 323–60.

Daybell, J. *The Material Letter in Early Modern England: Manuscript Letters and the Culture and Practices of Letter-Writing, 1512–1635*, Houndmills: Palgrave Macmillan, 2012.

DeFalco, A. 'Towards a Theory of Posthuman Care: Real Humans and Caring Robots', *Body & Society* 26.3 (2020), 31–60. https://doi.org/10.1177/1357034X20917450.

Dillen, A. ed., *Soft Shepherd or Almighty Pastor? Power and Pastoral Care*, Cambridge: James Clarke, 2015.

Dowling, E. *The Care Crisis: What Caused It and How Can We End It?*, London: Verso, 2021.

Ferlier, L. 'Building Religious Communities with Books: The Quaker and Anglican Transatlantic Libraries', M. Towsey & K. B. Roberts, eds., *Before the Public Library: Reading, Community and Identity in the Atlantic World, 1650–1850*, Leiden: Brill, 2018, 31–51.

Ferlier, L. 'George Keith (1639–1716), an Intellectual Geography of Tolerance from Presbyterian Scotland to Quaker Pennsylvania', *Global Intellectual History* 5:2 (2020), 210–30.

Fleming, J. *Cultural Graphology: Writing after Derrida*, Chicago: University of Chicago Press, 2016.

Foote, T. W. *Black and White Manhattan: The History of Racial Formation in Colonial New York City*, Oxford: Oxford University Press, 2004.

Foucault, M. *Security, Territory, Population: Lectures at the Collège de France 1977–1978*, trans. G. Burchell, Houndmills: Palgrave Macmillan, 2007.

Fuentes, M. J. *Dispossessed Lives: Enslaved Women, Violence, and the Archive*, Philadelphia: University of Pennsylvania Press, 2016.

Furey, C. *Erasmus, Contarini, and the Religious Republic of Letters*, Cambridge: Cambridge University Press, 2005.

Games, A. *The Web of Empire: English Cosmopolitans in an Age of Expansion, 1560–1660*, Oxford: Oxford University Press, 2008.

Gerbner, K. 'Antislavery in Print: The Germantown Protest, the "Exhortation", and the Seventeenth-Century Quaker Debate on Slavery', *Early American Studies* 9.3 (2011), 552–75.

Gerbner, K. *Christian Slavery: Conversion and Race in the Protestant Atlantic World*, Philadelphia: University of Pennsylvania Press, 2018.

Gikandi, S. *Slavery and the Culture of Taste*, Princeton: Princeton University Press, 2011.

Glasson, T. *Mastering Christianity: Missionary Anglicanism and Slavery in the Atlantic World*, Oxford: Oxford University Press, 2012.

Glickman, G. 'Protestantism, Colonization, and the New England Company in Restoration Politics', *The Historical Journal* 59.2 (2016), 365–91.

Golder, B. 'Foucault and the Genealogy of Pastoral Power', *Radical Philosophy Review* 10.2 (2007), 157–76.

Ha, P. 'Freedom of Association and Ecclesiastical Independence', M. Davies, A. Dunan-Page & J. Halcomb, eds., *Church Life: Pastors, Congregations and the Experience of Dissent in Seventeenth-Century England*, Oxford: Oxford University Press, 2019, 101–18.

Halcomb, J. 'The Association Movement and the Politics of Church Settlement in the Interregnum', E. Vernon & H. Powell, eds., *Church Polity and Politics in the British Atlantic World, c. 1635–66*, Manchester: Manchester University Press, 2020, 174–99.

Hall, A. D. 'Epistle, Meditation, and Sir Thomas Browne's *Religio Medici*', *PMLA* 94.2 (1979), 234–46.

Hall, D. D. 'Puritanism in a Local Context: Ministry, People, and Church in 1630s Massachusetts', U. Rublack, ed., *Protestant Empires: Globalizing the Reformations*, Cambridge: Cambridge University Press, 2020, 56–81.

Hardy, N. *Criticism and Confession: The Bible in the Seventeenth-Century Republic of Letters*, Oxford: Oxford University Press, 2017.

Harris, J. '"Heroick Virtue": Joseph Alleine's Letters and Protestant Martyrology', *Bunyan Studies* 23 (2019), 24–44.

Haslam, S. 'Reading, Trauma and Literary Caregiving 1914–1918: Helen Mary Gaskell and the War Library', *Journal of Medical Humanities* 41.3 (2018), 305-21. https://doi.org/10.1007/s10912-018-9513-5.

Haydon, L. D. *Corporate Culture: National and Transnational Corporations in Seventeenth-Century Literature*, London: Routledge, 2018.

Hughes, A. '"A Soul Preaching to Itself": Sermon Note-Taking and Family Piety', E. Clarke & R. W. Daniel, eds., *People and Piety: Protestant Devotional Identities in Early Modern England*, Manchester: Manchester University Press, 2020, 63–78.

Jennings, W. J. *The Christian Imagination: Theology and the Origins of Race*, New Haven: Yale University Press, 2010.

Johnson, J. M. *Wicked Flesh: Black Women, Intimacy, and Freedom in the Atlantic World*, Philadelphia: University of Pennsylvania Press, 2020.

Keeble, N. H. 'The Reformed Pastor as Nonconformist: Richard Baxter', M. Davies, A. Dunan-Page, & J. Halcombe, eds., *Church Life: Pastors, Congregations, and the Experience of Dissent in Seventeenth-Century England*, Oxford: Oxford University Press, 2019, 136–51.

Keeble, N. H. *Richard Baxter: Puritan Man of Letters*, Oxford: Clarendon Press, 1982.

Keeble, N. H. & G. F. Nuttall, *Calendar of the Correspondence of Richard Baxter*, Oxford: Clarendon Press, 1991, 2 vols.

Keeble, N. H., Coffey, J., Cooper, T., & Charlton, T., eds., *Richard Baxter: Reliquiae Baxterianae*, Oxford: Oxford University Press, 2020, 5 vols.

Kittay, E. F. 'The Ethics of Care, Dependence, and Disability', *Ratio Juris* 24.1 (2011), 49–58.

Kreitzer, L. 'Thomas Lambe the Linen Draper – Some New Evidence', E. Geldbach, ed., *Crossing Baptist Boundaries: A Festschrift in Honor of William Henry Brackney*, Macon: Mercer University Press, 2019, 209–20.

Laing, A. '"Heathens and Infidels"? African Christanization and Anglicanism in the South Carolina Low Country, 1700–1750', *Religion and American Culture* 12.2 (2002), 197–228.

Lynch, K. '"Letting a Room in a London-House": A Place for Dissent in Civil War London', M. Davies, A. Dunan-Page & J. Halcomb, eds., *Church Life: Pastors, Congregations and the Experience of Dissent in Seventeenth-Century England*, Oxford: Oxford University Press, 2019, 63–81.

Malay, J. 'Reassessing Anne Clifford's Books: The Discovery of a New Manuscript Inventory', *The Papers of the Bibliographical Society of America* 115.1 (2021), 1–41. https://doi.org/10.1086/712910.

Marshall, W. 'Tenison, Thomas (1636–1715), Archbishop of Canterbury'. *Oxford Dictionary of National Biography*. 23 September. 2004.

Mayes, C. 'Pastoral Power and the Confessing Subject in Patient-Centred Communication', *Journal of Bioethical Inquiry* 6.4 (2009), 483–93.

McKendry, A. *Disavowing Disability*, Cambridge: Cambridge University Press, 2021.

Miller, J. 'Medicines of the Soul: Reparative Reading and the History of Bibliotherapy', *Mosaic* 51.2 (2018), 17–34.

Mitchell, K. 'Identifying White Mediocrity and Know-Your-Place Aggression: A Form of Self-Care', *African American Review* 51.4 (2018), 253–62.

Mitchell, M. *The Prince of Slavers: Humphry Morice and the Transformation of Britain's Transatlantic Slave Trade, 1698–1732*, Cham: Palgrave Macmillan, 2020.

Mohamed, F. G. 'On Race and Historicism: A Polemic in Three Turns', *English Literary History* 89.2 (2022), 377–405.

More, E. 'Congregationalism and the Social Order: John Goodwin's Gathered Church, 1640–60', *The Journal of Ecclesiastical History* 38.2 (1987), 210–35.

Newton, H. *Misery to Mirth: Recovery from Illness in Early Modern England*, Oxford: Oxford University Press, 2018.

Norbrook, D. '"A Fleet of Worlds": Marvell, Globalisation, and Slavery', M. C. Augustine, G. J. Pertile & S. N. Zwicker, eds., *Imagining Andrew Marvell at 400*, British Academy: Oxford University Press, 2022, 88–108.

Oast, J. *Institutional Slavery: Slaveholding Churches, Schools, Colleges, and Businesses in Virginia, 1680–1860*, Cambridge: Cambridge University Press, 2016.

Pal, C. *Republic of Women: Rethinking the Republic of Letters in the Seventeenth Century*, Cambridge: Cambridge University Press, 2012.

Park, P. 'An Evolving History and Methodology of Pastoral Theology, Care, and Counseling', *Journal of Spirituality in Mental Health* 9.1 (2006), 5–33.

Perry, K. H. 'Black Futures Not Yet Lost: Imagining Black British Abolitionism', *The South Atlantic Quarterly* 121.3 (2022), 541–60.

Peters, K., Walsham, A. & Corens, L. eds., *Archives and Information in the Early Modern World*, Oxford: Oxford University Press, 2018.

Pettigrew, W. A. & Veevers, D. eds., *The Corporation as a Protagonist in Global History, c. 1550–1750*, Leiden: Brill, 2019.

Pullin, N. *Female Friends and the Making of Transatlantic Quakerism, 1650–1750*, Cambridge: Cambridge University Press, 2018.

Rosenberg, P. 'Thomas Tryon and the Seventeenth-Century Dimensions of Antislavery', *The William and Mary Quarterly* 61.4 (2004), 609–42.

Rublack, U. ed., *Protestant Empires: Globalizing the Reformations*, Cambridge: Cambridge University Press, 2020.

Russell, C. *Being a Jesuit in Renaissance Italy: Biographical Writing in the Early Global Age*, Harvard: Harvard University Press, 2022.

Schmidt, J. *Melancholy and the Care of the* Soul, London: Routledge, 2007.

Schneider, G. *Print Letters in Seventeenth-Century England: Politics, Religion, and News Culture*, London: Routledge, 2018.

Searle, A. & Vine, E. '"We Have Sick Souls When God's Physic Works Not": Samuel Rutherford's Pastoral Letters as a Form of Literary Cure', *The Seventeenth Century* 37.6 (2022), 913–36.

Siddique, A. 'The Archival Epistemology of Political Economy in the Early Modern British Atlantic World', *William & Mary Quarterly*, 77.4 (2020), 641–74.

Siddique, A. 'Governance through Documents: The Board of Trade, Its Archive, and the Imperial Constitution of the Eighteenth-Century British Atlantic', *Journal of British Studies* 59.2 (2020), 264–90.

Sirota, B. *The Christian Monitors: The Church of England and the Age of Benevolence, 1680–1730*, Yale: Yale University Press, 2014.

Sloane, A. *Vulnerability and Care: Christian Reflections on the Philosophy of Medicine*, London: T&T Clark, 2016.

Smith, B. 'Between the Galley and Plantation: The Rhetorical Construction of English Servants in the Seventeenth Century', *The Seventeenth Century* 38.1 (2023), 23–47.

Smith, H. 'Religion', W. A. Pettigrew & D. Veevers, eds., *The Corporation as a Protagonist in Global History, c. 1550–1750*, Leiden: Brill, 2019, 137–62.

Smith, J. D. 'Positioning Missionaries in Development Studies, Policy, and Practice', *World Development* 90 (2017), 63–76.

Speelman, G. 'Shifting Concepts of Pastoral Care in the Christian Tradition: From the Past to the Present to the Future', A. H. Grung, ed., *Complexities of Spiritual Care in Plural Societies: Education, Praxis and Concepts*, Berlin: De Gruyter, 2023, 15–32.

Steele, I. K. *The English Atlantic, 1675–1740: An Exploration of Communication and Community*, Oxford: Oxford University Press, 1986.

Sullivan, W. *A Ministry of Presence: Chaplaincy, Spiritual Care, and the Law*, Chicago: Chicago University Press, 2014.

Swift, C. *Hospital Chaplaincy in the Twenty-First Century: The Crisis of Spiritual Care on the NHS*, Aldershot: Ashgate, 2009.

Sytsma, D. *Richard Baxter and the Mechanical Philosophers*, Oxford: Oxford University Press, 2017.

Trigg, C. 'The Racial Politics of Resurrection in the Eighteenth-Century Atlantic World', *Early American Literature* 55.1 (2020), 47–84.

Tronto, J. C. 'An Ethic of Care', *Generations* 22.3 (1998), 15–20.

Vernon, E. 'Godly Pastors and Their Congregations in Mid-Seventeenth-Century London', M. Davies, A. Dunan-Page & J. Halcomb, eds., *Church Life: Pastors, Congregations and the Experience of Dissent in Seventeenth-Century England*, Oxford: Oxford University Press, 2019, 45–62.

Ward, M. *The Christian Quaker: George Keith and the Keithian Controversy*, Leiden: Brill, 2019.https://doi.org/10.1163/9789004396890

Warren, W. *New England Bound: Slavery and Colonization in Early America*, New York: W. W. Norton, 2016.

Winship, M. 'Defining Puritanism in Restoration England: Richard Baxter and Others Respond to "A Friendly Debate"', *The Historical Journal* 54.3 (2011), 689–715.

Yamamoto, K. *Taming Capitalism before Its Triumph: Public Service, Distrust, and 'Projecting' in Early Modern England*, Oxford: Oxford University Press, 2018.

Acknowledgements

For their expertise and assistance with the Baxter manuscripts at Dr Williams's Library and the extensive SPG archives at Lambeth Palace Library and the Bodleian Library, I am grateful to Jane Giscombe and Catherine Wakeling. The research for this project was funded by the Arts and Humanities Research Council, which facilitated interdisciplinary collaborations with Jo Sadgrove, Emily Vine, Tom Charlton, and Miranda Lewis, enabling ongoing conversations that have shaped my thinking, and this Element, in important ways. Several other colleagues and friends have offered encouragement, support, and wisdom at timely points, in particular, Johanna Harris, N. H. Keeble, Jason Kerr, Andrew Sloane, Andrew Warnes, and Rachel Willie. The series editors, Eve Tavor Bannet, Rebecca Bullard, and Markman Ellis, have provided critical and constructive support throughout the (lengthy) gestation process of this Element; the two anonymous readers modelled peer review and professional engagement in exceptionally generous and productive ways. Ian O'Harae helped me to have faith that I would find words to engage with the complex entanglements of pastoral care and power. Nathan and Antony Searle remind me daily that vulnerability, grace, accountability, and care are at the centre of what it means to not only write and think, but live well, and for that, I thank them.

About the Author

Alison Searle is Associate Professor of Textual Studies at the University of Leeds. Her research and publications focus on seventeenth-century epistolary culture, transatlantic puritan literary traditions, scholarly editing, pastoral care, the role of the imagination, and the relationship between literature and theology. She is also a general editor of *The Complete Correspondence of Richard Baxter* (forthcoming with Oxford University Press).

Cambridge Elements ⚎

Eighteenth-Century Connections

Elements in the Series

A full series listing is available at: www.cambridge.org/EECC